Fifty Fabulous Fables

Fifty Fabulous Fables

Beginning Readers Theatre

Suzanne I. Barchers

1997
TEACHER IDEAS PRESS
A Division of
Libraries Unlimited, Inc.
Englewood, Colorado

Dedicated to Donna Levene

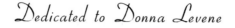

TEACHER IDEAS PRESS
A Division of
Libraries Unlimited, Inc.
P.O. Box 6633
Englewood, CO 80155-6633
(800) 237-6124
www.lu.com/tip

Production Editor: Stephen Haenel
Copy Editor: Beth Partin
Proofreader: Suzanne Hawkins Burke
Typesetter: Kay Minnis

Library of Congress Cataloging-in-Publication Data

Barchers, Suzanne I.
    Fifty fabulous fables : beginning readers theatre / Suzanne
I. Barchers.
      x, 139 p. 22x28 cm.
    Includes bibliographical references (p. 135) and index.
    Summary: A collection of theater scripts based on traditional fables from around the world and grouped according to reading levels.
    ISBN 1-56308-553-4
    1. Children's plays, American. 2. Fables--Adaptations.
3. Animals--Drama. [1. Plays. 2. Fables--Adaptations.
3. Animals--Drama.] I. Title.
PS3552.A5988F54   1997
812'.54--dc21   97-23132
                                                                            CIP
                                                                            AC

Contents

PART 3

PART 4

INTRODUCTION

THE ROLE OF READERS THEATRE

"Readers Theatre is a presentation by two or more participants who read from scripts and interpret a literary work in such a way that the audience imaginatively senses characterization, setting, and action. Voice and body tension rather than movement are involved, thus eliminating the need for the many practice sessions that timing and action techniques require in the presentation of a play" (Laughlin and Latrobe 1990, 3). Traditionally, the primary focus in readers theatre is on an effective reading of the script rather than on a dramatic, memorized presentation. Generally there are minimal props and movement on the stage, although with primary students, adding such touches enlivens the production and invites more active participation. The ease of incorporating readers theatre into the language arts program offers teachers an exciting way to enhance the program, especially in today's classrooms that emphasize a variety of reading and listening experiences.

Most of the scripts in this collection were developed from Aesop's fables. All scripts were evaluated with the Flesch-Kincaid readability scale and are grouped into sections with first-, second-, third-, or fourth-grade readability levels. Each script should be further evaluated by the teacher for features that will assist easy reading: familiarity, repetition, predictability, and so forth. In addition, some fables will be easy to read but will have concepts that are more difficult to understand.

Though children are not expected to memorize the lines in readers theatre, many children will have internalized the familiar story and will need only the slightest prompting from the script. Thus, paraphrasing by the reader is common and acceptable. Such success in reading and sharing is highly motivating for the beginning reader who appreciates the different form of reading. After spending an entire morning exploring and practicing a script, one second grader asked his teacher why they never had reading that day. She probed for a minute, then gently asked what they were doing as they prepared the script. He lit up in delight, "Oh, we *were* reading!"

The performance of readers theatre scripts also encourages strong oral skills for readers and promotes active listening for students in the audience (Sloyer 1982, 4). Students explore literature in a new form, and the class can begin to analyze various treatments of the same or similar stories through use of the related books or collections listed on pages 135–36. An additional benefit is the pleasure of performing for parents or other classes and the ease of preparing for special days when a program is expected.

PREPARING THE SCRIPTS

Once scripts are chosen for reading, make enough copies for each character, plus an extra set or two for your use and a replacement copy. Use highlighter markers to designate a character's lines within the copy. For example, the tortoise in "The Tortoise and the Hare" could be highlighted in blue each time it appears, the hare in green, and the narrator in orange. This helps readers track their parts and eases management of scripts in the event pages become mixed. Bold numbers are included in the right margin for easy prompting to a specific line by the teacher.

Photocopied scripts will last longer if you use three-hole punch or copy them on prepunched paper and place the scripts in an inexpensive folder. The folders can be color coordinated to the internal highlighting

This introduction is adapted from Suzanne I. Barchers, *Readers Theatre for Beginning Readers*. Englewood, CO: Teacher Ideas Press, 1993.

for each character's part. The title of the play can be printed on the outside of the folder, and scripts can be stored easily for the next reading. Preparing the scripts and folders is a good task for a volunteer parent or an older student helper. The preparation takes a minimum of initial attention and needs to be repeated only when a folder is lost.

GETTING STARTED

For the first experience with a readers theatre script, choose a script with many characters to involve as many students as possible. Gather the students informally, perhaps in a circle on the floor. Some of the more familiar fables are available in illustrated collections listed on pages 135–36. If an illustrated version is available, read it aloud to the students. Next, introduce the script version and explain that readers theatre does not mean memorizing a play and acting it out, but rather reading a script aloud with perhaps a few props and actions. Select volunteers to do the initial reading, allowing them an opportunity to review their parts before reading aloud. Other students could examine illustrated versions or brainstorm prop ideas and preview other scripts.

Before you read the first script, decide whether to choose parts after the reading or to introduce additional scripts to involve more students. A readers theatre workshop could be held periodically, with every student belonging to a group that prepares a script for presentation. A readers theatre festival could be planned for a special day when several short scripts would be presented consecutively, with brief intermissions between each reading. Groups of fables could include themes such as justice, revenge, greed, trickery, envy, foolishness, and so forth.

Once the students have read the scripts and become familiar with new vocabulary, determine which students will read the various parts. In assigning roles, strive for a balance between males and females. Many characters are animals and can be read by either sex. Some parts are considerably more demanding than others, and at first students should be encouraged to volunteer for roles that will be comfortable for them. Once they are familiar with readers theatre, students should be asked to try a reading that is challenging. Though one goal for incorporating readers theatre is to develop and inspire competent readers, it is equally important that the students succeed and enjoy the literature.

PRESENTATION SUGGESTIONS

For readers theatre, readers traditionally stand—or sit on stools, chairs, or the floor—in a formal presentation style. The narrator may stand with the script placed on a music stand or lectern slightly off to one side. The readers may hold their scripts in folders.

The position of the reader indicates the importance of the role. For example, the tortoise and the hare from the Aesop fable would be positioned to the front and center, with the narrator and starter to the back and side. When fables have several characters with brief parts, the characters may enter for their reading and then leave the stage. Alternatively, readers may stand up for a reading and sit down for the remainder of the script.

Because these scripts are for beginning readers, it is important that the students are comfortable with the physical arrangement. It is assumed that the students will present more informally, perhaps adapting or enlivening the presentation. Therefore, a traditional arrangement for presenters is not provided with the scripts. Instead, a few general suggestions are supplied for each play. Determining the presentation arrangement is a good cooperative activity for the readers. The arrangement should foster success: a student who cannot stand quietly for a long period of time should be allowed to sit on a chair, pillow, or the floor. The restless student reading a short part could remain onstage only for the duration of the reading. However, students may have fresh ideas for a different presentation, and their involvement should be fostered.

PROPS

Readers theatre traditionally has no, or few, props. However, simple costuming effects, such as a hat, apron, or scarf, plus a few props onstage will lend interest to the presentation. Shirlee Sloyer (1982, 58) suggests that a script can become a prop: "a book, a fan, a gun, or any other object mentioned in the story." Suggestions for simple props or costuming are included; however, encourage the students to decide how much or little to add to their production. They will get many good ideas from examining illustrated versions of the fables. It is possible that, for beginning readers, the use of props or actions may be overwhelming, and the emphasis should remain on the reading, rather than on an overly complicated presentation.

DELIVERY

In an effort to keep the scripts easy for beginning readers, no delivery suggestions are written within the scripts. Therefore, it is important to discuss with the students ways to make the scripts come alive as they read. Primary students naturally incorporate voices into their creative play and should be encouraged to explore how this same practice will enhance their reading. Small groups that are working on individual plays should be invited to brainstorm delivery styles. A variety of warm-ups can help students with expression. For example, have the entire class respond to the following:

- discovering school has been canceled due to snow

- being grounded for something a sibling did

- learning a best friend is moving

- getting a new puppy or kitten

- being told there will be a big test every Monday

- discovering a sister ate your last piece of birthday cake

- having a genie or fairy appear with three wishes

In their first experiences with presenting a script, students may keep their heads buried in the script, making sure they don't miss a line. Students should learn the material well enough to look up from the script during a presentation. Students can learn to use onstage focus, in which they focus on each other during the presentation. This is most logical for characters who are interacting with each other. The use of offstage focus, in which presenters look directly into the eyes of the audience, is more logical for the narrator or characters who are uninvolved with onstage characters. Students can also focus on a prearranged offstage location during delivery.

Simple actions can also be incorporated into readers theatre. Encourage students to use action by practicing pantomime in groups (primary students are generally less inhibited than older students). If possible, have a mime come in for a presentation and some introductory instruction, or introduce mime by having students try the following familiar actions: combing hair, brushing teeth, turning the pages of a book, eating an ice cream cone, making a phone call, or falling asleep. Then select and try general activities drawn from the scripts: climbing, carrying items, putting a hat on and taking it off, kneeling, and so forth. The actions need not be elaborate; characters can indicate falling asleep simply by closing their eyes. These minimal gestures and actions can brighten the presentations for both participants and audience.

Generally the audience should be able to see the readers' facial expressions during the reading. Upon occasion a script lends itself to a character moving across the stage, facing each character while reading. In this event the characters should be turned enough that the audience can see the readers' faces.

The use of music can enhance the delivery of the play. The sound of the wind could be added to "The Wind and the Sun." Royal music may be effective in "The Fox and the Monkey Who Was Elected King." A bell may tinkle during "Belling the Cat." As with props and action, music should be added sparingly so the emphasis can remain on the reading.

THE AUDIENCE

When students are part of the audience, they should understand their role. Caroline Feller Bauer (1992, 30) recommends that students should rehearse applauding and reacting appropriately to the script. Several of the plays can accommodate sound effects from the audience. Cue cards that prompt the audience to make noises can be incorporated into the production. Encourage students to find additional ways to involve the audience in the program.

BEYOND READERS THEATRE FOR BEGINNING READERS

Once students have enjoyed the reading process involved in preparing and presenting readers theatre, the next logical step is to involve them in the process of writing their own scripts. Several of the fables in this book occur in other versions, and suggestions for creating a contrasting version are given. The options for scripts are endless, and students will naturally want to translate a favorite story into a script. For an in depth discussion of this process, consult part 1 of Shirlee Sloyer's *Readers Theatre: Story Dramatization in the Classroom*.

REFERENCES

Bauer, Caroline Feller. 1992. *Read for the Fun of It: Active Programming with Books for Children*. Illustrated by Lynn Gates Bredeson. Bronx, NY: H. W. Wilson.

Laughlin, Mildred Knight, and Kathy Howard Latrobe. 1990. *Readers Theatre for Children: Scripts and Script Development*. Englewood, CO: Teacher Ideas Press, 1990.

Sloyer, Shirlee. 1982. *Readers Theatre: Story Dramatization in the Classroom*. Urbana, IL: National Council of Teachers of English.

PART 1

THE BAT, THE BIRDS, AND THE BEASTS

SUMMARY

A bat can't decide which army to join, the birds or the beasts. Because of her indecision, neither wants her later. (Aesop)

Reading level: 1.

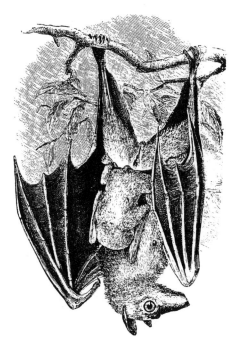

PRESENTATION SUGGESTIONS

This fable offers opportunities to have multiple readers for the birds and the beasts. The bat should be center stage, with the bird(s) on one side and the beast(s) on the other side. The narrator could stand on either side of the stage.

PROPS

Birds could wear colorful T-shirts. The beasts could be in more earthy colors. The bat could wear a black T-shirt.

DELIVERY

The birds and beasts should try to sound convincing, and the bat should sound indecisive.

CHARACTERS

📖	Narrator
BA	Bat
BI	Bird(s)
BE	Beast(s)

THE BAT, THE BIRDS, AND THE BEASTS

 Narrator: The birds and the beasts were going to have a fight. They both brought their armies to the war. Everyone was ready to fight except the bat.

BA   **Bat:** I don't know which army to join.   1

BI   **Birds:** Come with us. You fly through the air. You are a bird.   2

BA   **Bat:** But I'm also a beast.   3

    Narrator: The beasts heard him and called out.

BE   **Beasts:** Come with us then. Join our army.   4

BA   **Bat:** But I am a bird. I fly through the air.   5

    Narrator: Just then the leaders of both armies made peace. There would be no war after all. The bat joined the birds to celebrate.

BA   **Bat:** What good news! Let's have a party!   6

BI   **Birds:** But you said you weren't a bird! Go away!   7

    Narrator: The bat flew to the beasts and tried to join them.

BE   **Beasts:** Go away, bat! You said you were a bird!   8

    Narrator: So the bat flew away, but she had learned a valuable lesson.

BA   **Bat:** *She that is neither one thing nor another has no friends.*   9

BELLING THE CAT

SUMMARY

The mice live contentedly until a cat disrupts their freedom. They meet and decide to tie a ribbon with a bell attached on the cat. However, no one is willing to tackle the task. (Aesop)
Reading level: 1.

PRESENTATION SUGGESTIONS

This fable provides an opportunity to involve many students. The Other Mice have several lines in unison, and many students could share this role. The formal staging could include Narrator, Mouse Leader, and Young Mouse positioned stage front. Alternatively, the staging could have Mouse Leader on the side, raised on a chair or stool, with the others loosely arranged as in a meeting. An additional, nonspeaking role could be created for a cat who could simply prowl in the background.

PROPS

The mice could wear pink and gray ears on a headband made of felt and reinforced with interfacing. The leader could wear buttons or a hat to designate his role, and Wise Old Mouse could wear a tie. A ribbon and bell could be placed on stools onstage.

DELIVERY

Mouse Leader should have a strong voice. Other Mice could have squeaky and young voices. Young Mouse should sound young, and Wise Old Mouse should sound tentative. The audience could be prompted with cue cards to contribute mouse and cat sounds, and a bell could be rung softly when Young Mouse suggests belling the cat.

CHARACTERS

📖	Narrator	**YM**	Young Mouse
ML	Mouse Leader	**WM**	Wise Old Mouse
OM	Other Mice (as many as preferred)	**CA**	Cat (nonspeaking, optional)
HM	Hungry Mouse		

Excerpted from *Readers Theatre for Beginning Readers* by Suzanne I. Barchers. Englewood, CO: Teacher Ideas Press, 1993, p. 7.

BELLING THE CAT

Narrator: There were many mice living happily together in a big, old house. One day a cat arrived. After the mice were chased by the cat for some days, the leader of the mice called them together.

ML	**Mouse Leader:** My friends, we have a problem.	1
OM	**Other Mice:** What is it?	2
ML	**Mouse Leader:** It is that wicked cat! I am tired of being chased night and day.	3
HM	**Hungry Mouse:** Me too! I haven't had a crumb to eat since that beast came. I am so hungry!	4
OM	**Other Mice:** Me too! Me too!	5
ML	**Mouse Leader:** Well, we must come up with a plan. We have to be able to run about the house again.	6
OM	**Other Mice:** A plan! A plan!	7
YM	**Young Mouse:** I know what to do.	8
OM	**Other Mice:** What? What?	9
YM	**Young Mouse:** There is a bell in the corner of the kitchen and a ribbon in the bedroom. First, we have to put the bell on the ribbon. Then we wait for the cat to fall asleep and tie the ribbon around his neck. When he moves the bell will ring. We will be able to hear it and run away.	10
OM	**Other Mice:** Hurray! Hurray!	11

From *Fifty Fabulous Fables*. © 1997 Suzanne I. Barchers. Teacher Ideas Press. (800) 237-6124.

ML	**Mouse Leader:**	That is a splendid plan. Let's do it!	**12**
WM	**Wise Old Mouse:**	Excuse me, please.	**13**
ML	**Mouse Leader:**	What is it, old mouse? We have no time to waste!	**14**
WM	**Wise Old Mouse:**	Who is going to tie the bell around the cat's neck?	**15**
ML	**Mouse Leader:**	Why, a volunteer, of course.	**16**
WM	**Wise Old Mouse:**	And who will volunteer?	**17**

Narrator: The mice all looked at each other, waiting for someone to volunteer. No one did. And *mice are still caught by cats to this very day.*

THE DOG AND THE WOLF

SUMMARY

A wolf decides he wants to work in exchange for his meals, just like his friend the dog. Then he discovers that he will lose his freedom. (Aesop)
Reading level: 1.

PRESENTATION SUGGESTIONS

The narrator should stand to the side. The wolf could slip onto the stage, looking faint and weak, and meet the dog, who looks more lively. They could slowly move across the stage as they read and head toward town.

PROPS

Consider having the dog in black or brown clothing, perhaps with some padding to indicate his being well fed. The wolf could look more ragged and thin.

DELIVERY

The wolf should sound discouraged. The dog should sound happy but resigned to his lot, even though it involves being chained at night.

CHARACTERS

	Narrator
D	Dog
W	Wolf

THE DOG AND THE WOLF

📖 **Narrator:** A wolf was almost dead with hunger when he met a dog passing by.

D **Dog:** Hello, cousin. You don't look too good. I knew your bad habits would soon catch up to you. You should work like I do. Then your food would be given to you each day. **1**

W **Wolf:** I would like that, my friend. But where would I get such a job? **2**

D **Dog:** Let me help you. Come with me to my place. My master will let you share the work with me. **3**

📖 **Narrator:** The wolf and the dog went toward the town together. On the way, the wolf saw that the dog's hair was worn in one spot.

W **Wolf:** Why is your hair worn like that, my friend? **4**

D **Dog:** Oh that? That's nothing. That is where the master puts on the collar. **5**

W **Wolf:** But why does he put on a collar? **6**

D **Dog:** So he can chain me up at night. It hurts at first, but you get used to it. **7**

📖 **Narrator:** The wolf stopped and looked at the dog.

W **Wolf:** If that's what will happen just for a meal, then I must say goodbye. *It is better to starve free than to be a fat slave.* **8**

THE FOX AND THE CROW

SUMMARY

The fox tricks a crow into dropping its piece of cheese.
(Aesop)
Reading level: 1.

PRESENTATION SUGGESTIONS

This is a very short, simple tale that is especially appropriate for beginning readers. Because there are only three characters, it could be presented with another short fable, such as "The Wolf and the Crane" on page 37. To stage this fable, perch the crow on a stool with the fox looking up at it.

PROPS

For a whimsical treatment, the crow could have a piece of cheese in its mouth until it speaks, and the fox could have a felt tail.

DELIVERY

Because the crow's role is so small, it could shake its head in response to the fox's requests. The fox should sound alternatively pleading, flattering, and pompous.

CHARACTERS

 Narrator

F Fox

C Crow

THE FOX AND THE CROW

Narrator: One day a fox saw a crow fly by. The crow had a piece of cheese in its beak. Seeing the cheese made the fox very hungry. The crow came to rest on the branch of a tree.

F   **Fox:** Good morning, crow. Will you share your cheese with me?   **1**

Narrator: The crow looked at the fox. It slowly shook its head.

F   **Fox:** You look so kind. I am so hungry. Please share with me.   **2**

Narrator: The crow looked at the fox. Again it slowly shook its head.

F   **Fox:** You are the finest crow I have ever seen. Your feathers are so **3** black and glossy. You also have good luck by getting that cheese. Won't you share your good fortune with me?

Narrator: The crow looked at the fox. Again it slowly shook its head.

F   **Fox:** Your eyes are so bright. I am sure your voice must be every bit **4** as beautiful. Won't you sing for me? Then I will greet you as the Ruler of Birds.

Narrator: The crow could not resist such flattery.

C   **Crow:** Caw, caw, caw.   **5**

Narrator: As the crow sang, the cheese dropped to the ground. The fox gobbled it up.

C   **Crow:** You are a sneaky beast. One day your tricks will get you into **6** trouble. You should be taught a lesson.

F   **Fox:** That may be true. But you have learned a valuable lesson, crow. **7** *Do not trust a fox that flatters!*

From *Fifty Fabulous Fables*. © 1997 Suzanne I. Barchers. Teacher Ideas Press. (800) 237-6124.

THE FOX AND THE GOAT

SUMMARY

When a fox falls into a well, he tricks the goat into joining him. After using the goat to climb out, he leaves her behind. (Aesop)
Reading level: 1.

PRESENTATION SUGGESTIONS

The fox should have center stage, with the narrator off to one side. The goat should enter the stage for her lines. The fox could exit, leaving the goat and narrator behind at the end. Consider pairing this fable with others that have the fox as the main character.

PROPS

Consider using T-shirts, labels, a tail for the fox, and horns for the goat. Place a bucket and rope on the stage to portray a well.

DELIVERY

The fox should sound clever. The goat should sound innocent.

CHARACTERS

📖	Narrator
G	Goat
F	Fox

THE FOX AND THE GOAT

Narrator: A fox was walking along one day. He wasn't looking at where he was going and fell into a deep well. A goat was passing by and looked down into the well.

G	**Goat:** Fox, my friend. What are you doing in that well?	**1**
F	**Fox:** Haven't you heard? There is going to be a drought. I jumped down here so I could be near some water.	**2**
G	**Goat:** What a good idea! You are surely clever.	**3**
F	**Fox:** Why don't you jump down with me? Then you would be near water too.	**4**
G	**Goat:** Another good idea!	**5**
	Narrator: The goat jumped into the well. The fox then jumped right on her back.	
G	**Goat:** What are you doing? I thought we were down here to be near the water.	**6**
F	**Fox:** Oh, we are. But just a minute, friend.	**7**
	Narrator: That gave the fox just enough time to step on the goat's horns and jump right out of the well.	
G	**Goat:** Wait, fox. How will I get out?	**8**
F	**Fox:** Goodbye, my friend. Next time, remember this: *Never trust the advice of someone in trouble.*	**9**

From *Fifty Fabulous Fables*. © 1997 Suzanne I. Barchers. Teacher Ideas Press. (800) 237-6124.

THE FOX AND THE LION

SUMMARY

At first the fox is frightened of the lion. After he sees him several times, he is bold enough to visit with him. (Aesop)
Reading level: 1.

PRESENTATION SUGGESTIONS

The fox should have center stage in this script. The lion could move on and off the stage from opposite directions each time the fox sees him. This fable is understated and lacks the twist at the end that many fables have. Consider having the students rewrite the ending and the moral for a second presentation.

PROPS

Consider having the lion in gold clothing and the fox in red. A mural could portray the woods. The fox could lurk behind a stool or plant.

DELIVERY

The fox should sound scared and later conversational. The lion should sound kingly but not frightening.

CHARACTERS

📖	Narrator
F	Fox
L	Lion

THE FOX AND THE LION

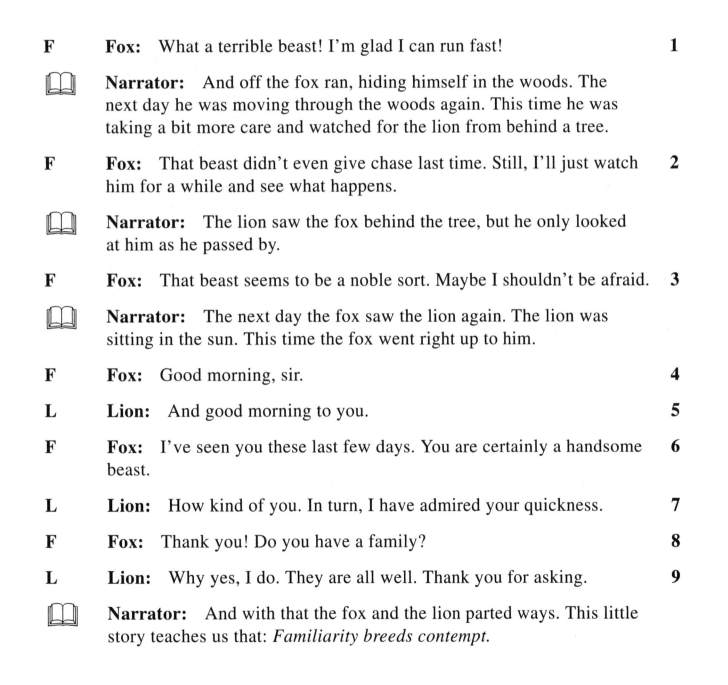

Narrator: The fox was walking along one fine day, enjoying the sun. All at once he saw a lion!

F   **Fox:** What a terrible beast! I'm glad I can run fast!   **1**

Narrator: And off the fox ran, hiding himself in the woods. The next day he was moving through the woods again. This time he was taking a bit more care and watched for the lion from behind a tree.

F   **Fox:** That beast didn't even give chase last time. Still, I'll just watch him for a while and see what happens.   **2**

Narrator: The lion saw the fox behind the tree, but he only looked at him as he passed by.

F   **Fox:** That beast seems to be a noble sort. Maybe I shouldn't be afraid.   **3**

Narrator: The next day the fox saw the lion again. The lion was sitting in the sun. This time the fox went right up to him.

F   **Fox:** Good morning, sir.   **4**

L   **Lion:** And good morning to you.   **5**

F   **Fox:** I've seen you these last few days. You are certainly a handsome beast.   **6**

L   **Lion:** How kind of you. In turn, I have admired your quickness.   **7**

F   **Fox:** Thank you! Do you have a family?   **8**

L   **Lion:** Why yes, I do. They are all well. Thank you for asking.   **9**

Narrator: And with that the fox and the lion parted ways. This little story teaches us that: *Familiarity breeds contempt.*

THE FROG AND THE OX

SUMMARY

When some young frogs are frightened by an ox, their father tries to prove that he can be as big as the ox. (Aesop)
Reading level: 1.

PRESENTATION SUGGESTIONS

The frogs could sit on the floor for this script, making it especially appropriate for children who have difficulty standing still. To involve more children, have two children read each frog's part. Place the narrator to the side. Have the father frog slightly to the other side, with the frogs placed so they appear to speak to him.

PROPS

Create lily pads for each frog to sit on. The frogs could wear green or brown T-shirts or have their numbers placed on their shirts. Students could draw murals for a marsh or pond setting.

DELIVERY

The young frogs should be scared and emphasize key words in the script. For example, when Young Frogs Four and Five say "Bigger, bigger, bigger," they should increase the volume. The father should sound irritated at their interruption at first, and then boastful.

CHARACTERS

📖	Narrator	YF3	Young Frog Three
FF	Father Frog	YF4	Young Frog Four
YF1	Young Frog One	YF5	Young Frog Five
YF2	Young Frog Two		

THE FROG AND THE OX

 Narrator: Some young frogs lived with their father in a pool.

YF1	**Young Frog One:** Oh, Father, I have just seen a monster!	1
FF	**Father Frog:** Hush, child, hush.	2
YF2	**Young Frog Two:** But, Father! I saw it too. It was as big as a mountain!	3
FF	**Father Frog:** Hush, child, hush.	4
YF3	**Young Frog Three:** But, Father! I saw it too. It had horns on its head.	5
FF	**Father Frog:** Horns on its head?	6
YF4	**Young Frog Four:** Yes, Father! And it had a long tail.	7
YF5	**Young Frog Five:** And it had hoofs divided in two.	8
FF	**Father Frog:** Hush, children, hush. That isn't a monster. It's the farmer's ox. He isn't so big.	9
YF1	**Young Frog One:** Yes, he is, Father! He's a monster!	10
FF	**Father Frog:** He may be taller. But I can make myself just as wide. Just watch!	11
	Narrator: The frog blew himself out and blew himself out and blew himself out. Then he stopped.	
FF	**Father Frog:** Was he as big as that?	12

**YF2
&
YF3**   **Young Frogs Two and Three:**   He was *much* bigger than that.   **13**

📖   **Narrator:**   So again the frog blew himself out and blew himself out and blew himself out.

FF   **Father Frog:**   Was he as big as that?   **14**

**YF4
&
YF5**   **Young Frogs Four and Five:**   Bigger, bigger, bigger!   **15**

📖   **Narrator:**   So the frog took a deep breath and blew as hard as he could. Just as he was going to ask the frogs if he was now as big as the ox, he burst. The frogs never forgot this lesson: *Self-conceit may lead to self-destruction.*

From *Fifty Fabulous Fables*. © 1997 Suzanne I. Barchers. Teacher Ideas Press. (800) 237-6124.

THE FROGS WHO WANTED A KING

SUMMARY

In spite of their idyllic life in the marsh, four frogs want a king. When they appeal to Jove and get their wish, they discover that life without rule is preferable. (Aesop)
Reading level: 1.

PRESENTATION SUGGESTIONS

The narrator could stand to the side with the frogs across the stage in the order of their speaking. The script doesn't call for the stork to speak, but a stork could be added at the end of the play, neatly "gobbling" each frog in turn. Similarly, Jove could be dressed as a supreme ruler, sitting to one side.

PROPS

Label the frogs as Frog One, Frog Two, and so forth. The stork could have a long paper beak if it is included in the staging. Jove could have a scepter or crown. A marsh scene could be created with drawings of cattails, reeds, lily pads, and so forth. If they are available, use green plants and a log onstage.

DELIVERY

The frogs should generally sound conversational.

CHARACTERS

📖	Narrator	**F5**	Frog Five
F1	Frog One	**F6**	Frog Six
F2	Frog Two	**JO**	Jove (nonspeaking, optional)
F3	Frog Three	**ST**	Stork (nonspeaking, optional)
F4	Frog Four		

THE FROGS WHO WANTED A KING

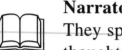 **Narrator:** The frogs lived a happy life in the marsh. They splashed and swam and played. But some frogs thought they should have more order in their lives.

F1 **Frog One:** All this splashing and swimming is fun. But shouldn't we be doing more? 1

F2 **Frog Two:** You're right. We need a king. Then there would be some order in this marsh. 2

F3 **Frog Three:** That's right. But how can we get a king? 3

F4 **Frog Four:** Let's ask Jove to send us one. 4

Narrator: The four frogs ask Jove to send them a king.

F1, F2, F3, & F4 **Frogs One, Two, Three, and Four:** Mighty Jove, send us a king. 5

Narrator: Jove thought they must be joking. He threw a huge log into the swamp. At first the frogs were all scared. Then they hopped up nearby to look at it.

F1 **Frog One:** Can this be our king? 6

F2 **Frog Two:** It's very big. 7

F3 **Frog Three:** But it doesn't even move! 8

F4 **Frog Four:** I'm going to touch it. Maybe it's asleep. 9

From *Fifty Fabulous Fables*. © 1997 Suzanne I. Barchers. Teacher Ideas Press. (800) 237-6124.

| | **Narrator:** But the log didn't move. The frogs even jumped up and down on it. It didn't move. Some of the frogs didn't care about having a king. They spoke up. | |

F5   **Frog Five:**   Look what Jove sent you! It doesn't do anything.   **10**

F6   **Frog Six:**   Forget about having a king. Just enjoy splashing and swimming.   **11**

Narrator: But the other frogs wanted a king more than ever. They tried again.

F1, F2,
F3, &
F4   **Frogs One, Two, Three, and Four:**   Mighty Jove, send us a king.   **12**

Narrator: This time Jove decided to teach them a lesson. He sent them a big stork. By the time the frogs realized their mistake, it was too late. The stork ate them all up. So remember, my friends: *Better no rule than cruel rule.*

From *Fifty Fabulous Fables*. © 1997 Suzanne I. Barchers. Teacher Ideas Press. (800) 237-6124.

THE HARE WITH MANY FRIENDS

SUMMARY

A popular hare discovers that when she is in trouble she really doesn't have reliable friends. (Aesop)
Reading level: 1.

PRESENTATION SUGGESTIONS

This script is especially effective because it uses several students and has repetitive language. Consider having the appropriate animals exit the stage after they finish their lines, or have all the animals stay onstage and have the hare move to each animal in turn. Students could add more animals to expand the script.

PROPS

Consider having the animals wear T-shirts with selected colors for the animals, or have them use labels for identification. A farm scene could be created with a mural, hay, and so forth.

DELIVERY

The hare should sound increasingly panicky. The animals should sound indifferent to her plight.

CHARACTERS

📖	Narrator	**G**	Goat
HA	Hare	**R**	Ram
HO	Horse	**C**	Calf
B	Bull		

THE HARE WITH MANY FRIENDS

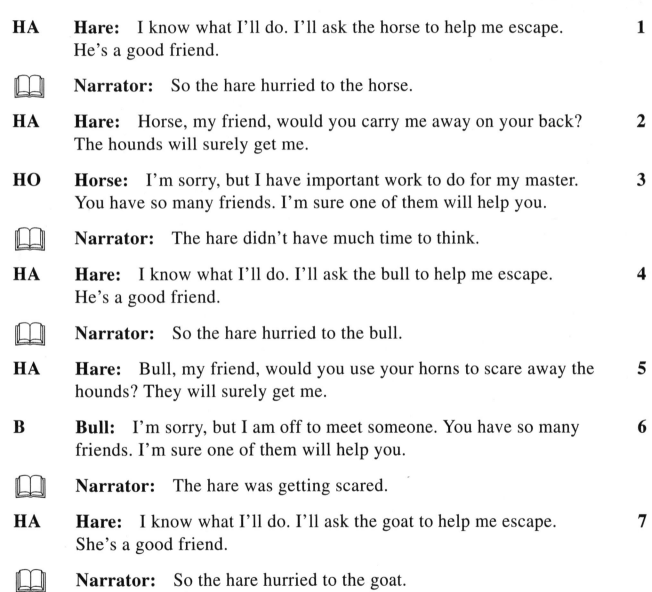

Narrator: A hare was quite popular. Many animals said they were her best friend. One day she heard the hounds approaching.

HA   **Hare:** I know what I'll do. I'll ask the horse to help me escape. He's a good friend.   **1**

Narrator: So the hare hurried to the horse.

HA   **Hare:** Horse, my friend, would you carry me away on your back? The hounds will surely get me.   **2**

HO   **Horse:** I'm sorry, but I have important work to do for my master. You have so many friends. I'm sure one of them will help you.   **3**

Narrator: The hare didn't have much time to think.

HA   **Hare:** I know what I'll do. I'll ask the bull to help me escape. He's a good friend.   **4**

Narrator: So the hare hurried to the bull.

HA   **Hare:** Bull, my friend, would you use your horns to scare away the hounds? They will surely get me.   **5**

B   **Bull:** I'm sorry, but I am off to meet someone. You have so many friends. I'm sure one of them will help you.   **6**

Narrator: The hare was getting scared.

HA   **Hare:** I know what I'll do. I'll ask the goat to help me escape. She's a good friend.   **7**

Narrator: So the hare hurried to the goat.

HA	**Hare:** Goat, my friend, would you butt the hounds away? They will surely get me.	**8**
G	**Goat:** I'm sorry, but I don't want to hurt my back. You have so many friends. I'm sure one of them will help you.	**9**
📖	**Narrator:** The hare was getting more scared.	
HA	**Hare:** I know what I'll do. I'll ask the ram to help me escape. He's a good friend.	**10**
📖	**Narrator:** So the hare hurried to the ram.	
HA	**Hare:** Ram, my friend, would you kick the hounds away? They will surely get me.	**11**
R	**Ram:** I'm sorry, but hounds have been known to eat sheep. You have so many friends. I'm sure one of them will help you.	**12**
📖	**Narrator:** The hare was running out of hope.	
HA	**Hare:** I know what I'll do. I'll ask calf to help me escape. She's a good friend.	**13**
📖	**Narrator:** So the hare hurried to the calf.	
HA	**Hare:** Calf, my friend, would you help me escape the hounds? The horse, bull, goat, and ram couldn't help me. You are my only friend left. The hounds will surely get me.	**14**
C	**Calf:** I'm sorry, but if none of them would help you, I don't see how I can take the risk.	**15**
📖	**Narrator:** By this time the hounds were very close.	
HA	**Hare:** I guess I just have to rely on myself to escape.	**16**
📖	**Narrator:** And fortunately, the hare did just that, proving that: *She who has many friends has no friends.*	

From *Fifty Fabulous Fables.* © 1997 Suzanne I. Barchers. Teacher Ideas Press. (800) 237-6124.

THE LION AND THE MOUSE

SUMMARY

A sleeping lion awakens because a mouse is using him as a playground. The lion agrees to let the mouse go. After hunters capture the lion, the mouse returns the favor by chewing through the lion's ropes. (Aesop)
Reading level: 1.

PRESENTATION SUGGESTIONS

Because this fable is very short and has only three characters, it could be paired with other lion fables. Staging could be formal, with characters sitting on stools or standing.

PROPS

The mouse could have a headband with pink and gray felt ears reinforced with interfacing. The lion could have a swishing tail of rope and whiskers of eyeliner pencil. A tree or plant could be in the background.

DELIVERY

The mouse should have a small and squeaky voice. The lion should sound big and gruff.

CHARACTERS

📖	Narrator
L	Lion
M	Mouse

Excerpted from *Readers Theatre for Beginning Readers* by Suzanne I. Barchers. Englewood, CO: Teacher Ideas Press, 1993, p. 14.

THE LION AND THE MOUSE

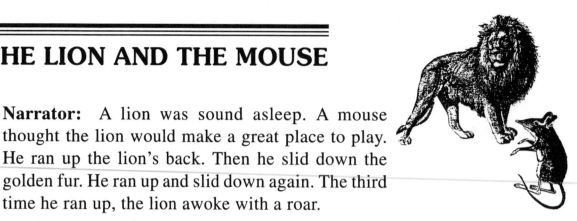

Narrator: A lion was sound asleep. A mouse thought the lion would make a great place to play. He ran up the lion's back. Then he slid down the golden fur. He ran up and slid down again. The third time he ran up, the lion awoke with a roar.

L   **Lion:** ROAR! What is this? Who is playing on my back?   1

M   **Mouse:** Oops!   2

Narrator: The lion looked around. Seeing the mouse, he used his tail to pull the mouse to his mouth.

L   **Lion:** Looks like a tasty treat!   3

M   **Mouse:** Please forgive me, King Lion. I was only having some fun.   4

L   **Lion:** The fun is over for you!   5

M   **Mouse:** Wait! I won't be much of a meal for such a big lion. Let me go. Someday I will pay you back. Please?   6

L   **Lion:** Hmmph! I can't think how you could ever pay me back. But it is true. You are not even a mouthful. Be off with you, then. Don't bother me again!   7

Narrator: The lion was soon asleep again. He did not hear some hunters creep up on him. Before he could even roar, they tied him to a tree. The hunters left to get a wagon to take the lion to the king. The lion roared his anger and fear at being trapped.

M   **Mouse:** That sounds like the lion! Why is he so upset? I'll go see what is wrong.   8

Narrator: The mouse found the lion tied to the tree.

From *Fifty Fabulous Fables.* © 1997 Suzanne I. Barchers. Teacher Ideas Press. (800) 237-6124.

M **Mouse:** Be quiet, my friend. Now I can pay you back. **9**

L **Lion:** How is that? I need more help than a tiny mouse can give. **10**

Narrator: But the mouse did not reply. He began to chew the ropes with his sharp little teeth. Soon the ropes fell away.

M **Mouse:** Now you are free, King Lion. Run before the hunters return. **11**

L **Lion:** I may be free. But you have proved to me that: *Little friends can be the best.* **12**

Narrator: From that day forth the lion and mouse were always friends.

THE MAN AND THE BEAST

SUMMARY

When a lost, cold man is rescued by a beast, he learns not to blow hot and cold with the same breath. (Aesop)

Reading level: 1.

PRESENTATION SUGGESTIONS

The man should be center stage with the narrator and beast on either side. The man could shiver and act cold in the beginning. To add more movement, the man and beast could walk onstage as the narrator reads the opening lines.

PROPS

Dress the man in a jacket and scarf. The beast could have makeup or costuming that would indicate a beast.

DELIVERY

The man should sound cold and frightened. The beast should sound gruff and somewhat impatient.

CHARACTERS

📖	Narrator
B	Beast
M	Man

THE MAN AND THE BEAST

Narrator: The night was cold and windy. A man had lost his way in the forest and was close to dying. A beast came along and found him.

B	**Beast:** You look like you could use some help.	**1**
M	**Man:** I have been lost for many hours, and I am cold and hungry.	**2**
B	**Beast:** Come to my den. I will give you a warm place to sleep and a fine stew to eat. In the morning I will lead you out of the forest.	**3**

Narrator: As they went along to the beast's den, the man raised his hands and blew on them.

B	**Beast:** Why do you do that?	**4**
M	**Man:** Why do I do what?	**5**
B	**Beast:** Why do you blow on your hands?	**6**
M	**Man:** My hands are numb with cold. My breath warms them.	**7**

Narrator: Soon they arrived at the beast's den. The beast prepared a steaming bowl of stew and gave it to the man. The man's mouth began to water from the fine smell of it.

M	**Man:** This stew smells fine. I owe you so much for bringing me to a place of warmth and comfort. I surely would have died without your kindness.	**8**

Narrator: The man raised a spoonful of stew to his mouth and began blowing on it.

B	**Beast:** Why do you do that?	**9**

M	**Man:**	Do what?	**10**
B	**Beast:**	Blow on the stew.	**11**
M	**Man:**	The stew is too hot, and my breath will cool it.	**12**
B	**Beast:**	Out you go!	**13**
M	**Man:**	But why?	**14**
B	**Beast:**	I will have nothing to do with a man who can blow hot and cold with the same breath.	**15**

Narrator: And that is why *wise men know not to blow hot and cold.*

THE TORTOISE AND THE HARE

SUMMARY

The hare brags that he can win any race. When the tortoise challenges him, the overconfident hare naps and consequently loses the race. (Aesop)

Reading level: 1.

PRESENTATION SUGGESTIONS

Consider combining the reading of this script with other short fables in this section. Staging could be formal, with characters standing or sitting on stools. To involve more students, consider assigning the roles to two sets of students, with the second set pantomiming the fable in front of the readers.

PROPS

Consider giving the hare long ears and tennis shoes. The tortoise could wear padded clothes and boots to indicate heaviness. The starter could have a stopwatch around his or her neck.

DELIVERY

The hare should speak boastfully and quickly. The tortoise should speak quietly and deliberately. The starter should have a commanding voice. The audience could be directed to join in with "On your marks. Get set. GO!"

CHARACTERS

📖	Narrator
H	Hare
T	Tortoise
S	Starter

Excerpted from *Readers Theatre for Beginning Readers* by Suzanne I. Barchers. Englewood, CO: Teacher Ideas Press, 1993, p. 25.

THE TORTOISE AND THE HARE

 Narrator: Once there were a tortoise and a hare. The tortoise was slow and careful. The hare did everything fast. He loved to brag about his speed.

H	**Hare:** I am so fast! I have never been beaten in a race. There isn't anyone who can beat me! In fact, no one is brave enough to try.	1
T	**Tortoise:** I am brave enough. I will race you.	2
H	**Hare:** You! That is a fine joke. I could run circles around you and still win the race!	3
T	**Tortoise:** You should save your bragging until you've won.	4
H	**Hare:** Let's race then!	5

 Narrator: The tortoise and the hare agreed on a race course. They would race on the path that led through the woods. All the animals lined up to watch.

S	**Starter:** Quiet! Quiet! It is time for the race. You know the rules. The first to cross the finish line is the winner. Tortoise, are you ready?	6
T	**Tortoise:** Yes, I am.	7
S	**Starter:** Hare, are you ready?	8
H	**Hare:** Of course! This will be a quick race!	9

From *Fifty Fabulous Fables*. © 1997 Suzanne I. Barchers. Teacher Ideas Press. (800) 237-6124.

S   **Starter:**   On your marks. Get set. GO!   **10**

Narrator: The tortoise got off to a steady start. The hare left a trail of dust as he raced off down the path.

T   **Tortoise:**   Oh, dear! Look at the hare go. I shouldn't have been so   **11**
brave. But there is no going back, only forward.

Narrator: The tortoise plodded on, hardly lifting his head to look down the path. Meanwhile, the hare stopped to look back at the tortoise. He waited and waited but didn't see him.

H   **Hare:**   This is too boring. I think I'll take a bit of a nap. That tortoise   **12**
won't be along for hours.

Narrator: The tortoise plodded on. The hare slept on. Finally, the tortoise neared the finish line. His animal friends began to cheer.

H   **Hare:**   What? What is all that noise? It must be time to finish the   **13**
race.

Narrator: But it was too late for the hare. The tortoise crossed the finish line just as the hare came around the last turn. As the animals cheered, the tortoise had only one thing to say to the hare.

T   **Tortoise:**   *Slow and steady wins the race.*   **14**

THE TOWN MOUSE AND THE COUNTRY MOUSE

SUMMARY

Two mice cousins visit each other's homes and find that both city and country have their drawbacks. (Aesop)
Reading level: 1.

PRESENTATION SUGGESTIONS

Staging could be formal, with the two mice taking center stage. The cook could enter and exit for her reading. A second set of students could pantomime the play while the others read. Because the mice are often thought of as male, it would be suitable to have variations, with females for one portrayal or mixed roles for the mice.

PROPS

The town mouse should be in dress clothes. The country mouse should be dressed casually, perhaps in tennis shoes, a T-shirt, and jeans. The town mouse could have an elegant suitcase nearby, and the country mouse could have a battered bag or bundle on a stick. The cook could wear a hat or apron. The cat could have felt ears, whiskers, tail, or collar.

DELIVERY

The town mouse should sound sophisticated and elegant, while the country mouse should sound simple. The cook should sound outraged, and the cat should sound eager to eat the mice.

CHARACTERS

	Narrator	**C**	Cook
TM	Town Mouse	**MC**	Mouser the Cat
CM	Country Mouse		

Excerpted from *Readers Theatre for Beginning Readers* by Suzanne I. Barchers. Englewood, CO: Teacher Ideas Press, 1993, p. 28.

THE TOWN MOUSE AND THE COUNTRY MOUSE

Narrator: One day the town mouse decided to visit his cousin in the country. The mice had a good chat. They had a breakfast of nuts and seeds. For lunch they had a picnic of nuts and seeds. The country mouse baked nuts and seeds for dinner. The town mouse soon tired of eating nuts and seeds.

TM **Town Mouse:** Cousin, come visit me in the city. I am tired of this simple food. I promise you that we will dine on the finest meats and cakes. 1

CM **Country Mouse:** That sounds splendid! When shall we go? 2

TM **Town Mouse:** Let's go now. I am ready to be home. 3

Narrator: The country mouse packed a simple bag. After some time they came near the city.

TM **Town Mouse:** We are almost home! I will be so happy to have real food! 4

Narrator: The mice came to a huge house. The town mouse led the country mouse to a small opening in the bricks in the back.

TM **Town Mouse:** Shhh! Now you must be as quiet as a whisper. 5

CM **Country Mouse:** Why? 6

TM **Town Mouse:** Never mind. Just be quiet. 7

Narrator: The town mouse led the country mouse into the dining room. They scampered up on the table. The table was littered with the remains of a fine feast.

TM **Town Mouse:** Now you see how I eat! Help yourself to anything you wish. 8

CM   Country Mouse: This is great! No wonder you wanted to come   **9**
home.

Narrator: The mice were enjoying second helpings when the
kitchen door opened.

C   Cook: Eeeek! Mice! Now there are two! Where is that pesky cat?   **10**
Mouser! Mouser! Where are you?

TM   Town Mouse: Time to run, cousin. Follow me!   **11**

Narrator: The town mouse led the country mouse to a hole under
the floor.

CM   Country Mouse: Who was that?   **12**

TM   Town Mouse: That is the cook. Don't worry about her. She is   **13**
harmless. She'll go back to the kitchen. Then we'll have dessert.

Narrator: Soon it was quiet again. The town mouse led the country
mouse back to the dining table.

TM   Town Mouse: Eat, my friend, eat. You won't find such sweet cakes   **14**
in the country.

Narrator: But just then, Mouser the cat leaped onto the table. One
paw landed on the country mouse's tail.

MC   Mouser the Cat: What have I here? Looks like dessert! Mrowr!   **15**

TM   Town Mouse: Run, cousin! Run! Meet me below!   **16**

Narrator: But the country mouse had seen enough. He twitched
his tail away from the cat. Then he darted toward the door.

CM   Country Mouse: No thanks, cousin! If this is life in the city, it is not   **17**
for me. I'll take my seeds and nuts any day. Goodbye! From now on,
you come and visit me!

Narrator: And that is why *the town mouse has to go to the country
to see his cousin.*

THE WOLF AND THE CRANE

SUMMARY

When a wolf gets a bone stuck in his throat, he promises a reward to the crane for removing the bone. Once the crane removes the bone, the wolf declares her safety is adequate reward. (Aesop)
Reading level: 1.

PRESENTATION SUGGESTIONS

The narrator should stand off to the side. The wolf should be in the center, with the crane between the wolf and the narrator. Place the other characters to the other side of the wolf. Those playing the lamb and deer may want to exit after their readings. To lengthen the play, consider adding other animals that refuse to help the wolf. Students could also consider acting out this script once it has been shared in readers theatre form.

PROPS

The animals could have simple costumes: paper headbands with appropriate ears, name cards that identify the animals, colors of T-shirts that match the animals, such as brown, black, and white.

DELIVERY

The wolf should sound desperate and ingratiating. The animals, except for the crane, should sound intimidated by the wolf.

CHARACTERS

	Narrator
W	Wolf
L	Lamb
D	Deer
C	Crane

THE WOLF AND THE CRANE

Narrator: A wolf was eating an animal he had killed. A small bone got stuck in his throat. He tried to swallow it. No luck. He tried to spit it up. No luck. He ran up the road, howling with pain.

W	**Wolf:** Ouch! Ouch! Ouch! I can't get this bone out.	1
📖	**Narrator:** The wolf ran down the road. He came to a lamb.	
W	**Wolf:** Lamb, would you help get this bone out?	2
L	**Lamb:** Not me, wolf. You would only make a meal of me.	3
📖	**Narrator:** The wolf ran down the road. He came to a deer.	
W	**Wolf:** Deer, would you help get this bone out?	4
D	**Deer:** Not me, wolf. You would only make a meal of me.	5
📖	**Narrator:** The wolf ran down the road. He came to a crane.	
W	**Wolf:** Crane, would you help get this bone out?	6
C	**Crane:** Why should I?	7
W	**Wolf:** You have a long beak. That would make the job easy.	8
C	**Crane:** But what will you give me?	9
W	**Wolf:** I would give *anything* if you would take it out.	10
📖	**Narrator:** The crane put its long neck down the wolf's throat and took out the bone.	
C	**Crane:** Now, what is my reward?	11
W	**Wolf:** You put your head inside a wolf's mouth. Then you safely took it out. That is reward enough for you.	12
C	**Crane:** I should have known better than to help a wolf.	13
📖	**Narrator:** So, dear listeners, this story again reminds us that: *Gratitude and greed do not go together.*	

From *Fifty Fabulous Fables*. © 1997 Suzanne I. Barchers. Teacher Ideas Press. (800) 237-6124.

THE WOLF AND THE KID

SUMMARY

A kid takes advantage of being in a safe place and taunts a wolf. (Aesop)

Reading level: 1.

PRESENTATION SUGGESTIONS

Have the narrator stand on one side of the stage. Place the kid in the center on something that raises it above the wolf, perhaps a stool or table. To contrast two tales about wolves, consider presenting this tale with "The Wolf and the Lamb" from Part 2. After the presentation, students could discuss the wolf's real intentions in this story.

PROPS

In addition to the table or chair for the kid, consider props that could indicate a countryside: plants, mural of trees and bushes, a road, and so forth.

DELIVERY

The kid should sound confident. The wolf should sound wheedling and frustrated.

CHARACTERS

📖   Narrator

K   Kid

W   Wolf

THE WOLF AND THE KID

Narrator: As you may know, goat kids make fine climbers. One day a kid had climbed to the top of its master's house. It was enjoying the view when it saw a wolf below.

Kid: Look who's here! It's the wolf again. 1

Wolf: I heard that. It's that kid. Just what I need for my dinner. Now where are you? 2

Kid: Look up and you'll see me. 3

Wolf: Now how did you get up there? 4

Kid: Mr. Wolf, you know that goats make great climbers. 5

Narrator: The wolf knew that unless he got the kid to come down he would go home hungry.

Wolf: Don't you think you should come down here where we can visit properly? 6

Kid: Ha! I'd never come down while you're nearby. You are a murderer and a thief. Everyone knows just how evil you are. 7

Wolf: You must be talking about my brother. You'd be quite safe with me. 8

Kid: You just go find someone else to trick, you ugly beast. 9

Wolf: You can say all you wish from that rooftop, my friend. But just remember: *It's easy to be brave from a safe distance.* 10

From *Fifty Fabulous Fables*. © 1997 Suzanne I. Barchers. Teacher Ideas Press. (800) 237-6124.

PART 2

THE BELLY AND THE MEMBERS OF THE BODY

SUMMARY

The members of the body decide that they are doing all the work while the belly enjoys all the food. They decide to strike, but they soon find that the belly is indeed sharing the load. (Aesop)

Reading level: 2.

PRESENTATION SUGGESTIONS

Ideal for combining with a unit on nutrition, this fable could easily be changed to have multiple readers for the body parts, such as the hands, teeth, and legs. Have the narrator stand to the side and arrange the speakers in the order of their parts.

PROPS

Because there are several speakers and the audience may lose track of which body part is speaking, consider providing labels. Alternatively, consider having the students use clown makeup to highlight the body part being represented (when practical).

DELIVERY

The characters should sound annoyed with the belly at first. Later they should sound tired.

CHARACTERS

📖	Narrator
H	Hands
M	Mouth
TE	Teeth
TH	Throat
L	Legs

THE BELLY AND THE MEMBERS OF THE BODY

Narrator: The members of the body decided that the belly wasn't doing any of the work.

H	**Hands:** I do so much work. I take the food and put it in the mouth.	1
M	**Mouth:** I do a lot of work too. I take the food so the teeth can chew it.	2
TE	**Teeth:** My work is hard. I chew the food so the throat can swallow it.	3
TH	**Throat:** And when I swallow, I get the food to the belly.	4
L	**Legs:** Don't forget us. Sometimes I take the body to where the food is.	5
H	**Hands:** But then the belly does nothing.	6
M	**Mouth:** Maybe we should just quit.	7
TE	**Teeth:** I could sure use a rest.	8
TH	**Throat:** Me, too. Let's go on strike!	9
L	**Legs:** That's fine with us!	10

Narrator: And so the members of the body quit working. The belly had to quit too. At first they were happy with their easy lives. But after a day or two they weren't quite as happy.

H	**Hands:** I can hardly move. I'm so tired.	11
M	**Mouth:** I am so dry. I really need some water.	12

From *Fifty Fabulous Fables*. © 1997 Suzanne I. Barchers. Teacher Ideas Press. (800) 237-6124.

TE	**Teeth:**	There sure isn't much to do.	**13**
TH	**Throat:**	Something cool would feel good to me.	**14**
L	**Legs:**	I can hardly stand up any more.	**15**
H	**Hands:**	Maybe the belly did help us.	**16**
M	**Mouth:**	I think so. The belly did digest the food.	**17**
TE	**Teeth:**	At least I had something to do then.	**18**
TH	**Throat:**	And I had the energy to swallow the food.	**19**
L	**Legs:**	All that food gave us energy too. I could get us wherever we needed to go!	**20**

Narrator: And so the members of the body decided that the belly was working after all. From that day forward, *the members of the body all worked together.*

THE CAT MAIDEN

SUMMARY

Jupiter and Venus argue over whether someone can change. When they put the argument to a test, Venus wins the dispute. (Aesop)
Reading level: 2.

PRESENTATION SUGGESTIONS

Venus and Jupiter should be center stage with the narrator off to one side.

PROPS

Consider adding a stuffed mouse and cat to the stage. Venus and Jupiter could be dressed to look regal.

DELIVERY

Venus and Jupiter should have strong voices and sound argumentative.

CHARACTERS

	Narrator
J	Jupiter
V	Venus

THE CAT MAIDEN

Narrator: The gods were arguing about whether it was possible for a living being to change its nature.

J	**Jupiter:** Yes, of course, it is possible for someone to change.	1
V	**Venus:** No, I don't agree with you. But let's put this to the test.	2
J	**Jupiter:** All right! I will change a cat into a maiden and marry her to a man. We'll see what happens.	3

Narrator: After the wedding, the young couple sat down at the wedding feast.

J	**Jupiter:** Look at how lovely she is. She behaves just like a young woman. No one could tell that she used to be a cat.	4
V	**Venus:** Wait a minute. I have a little test for her.	5

Narrator: Venus let a mouse loose in the room. As soon as she saw the mouse, the bride jumped up from her seat and tried to pounce on it.

V	**Venus:** See, my friend. I was right. *One cannot change nature.*	6

THE DEER IN THE BARN

SUMMARY

A deer being chased by hunters takes refuge in a barn. It escapes the hunters, but when the master discovers the deer, the stable boys kill it. (Aesop)
Reading level: 2.

PRESENTATION SUGGESTIONS

Have the narrator stand off to one side. Place the deer in the center with the master between the narrator and the deer. The stable boys, resting sleepily against a chair, could sit on the other side of the deer. Have the hunters come onstage for their lines and leave thereafter. The hunters could include as many readers as is practical.

PROPS

The deer could wear antlers made with felt-covered wire and stitched or glued onto a headband. (Watch for antler head wear during holiday sales.) The stable boys could be in work shirts, with the hunters wearing orange vests or red plaid. The master could be well dressed.

DELIVERY

The hunters should sound aggressive. The stable boys should sound somewhat bewildered. The master should sound bossy.

CHARACTERS

📖	Narrator	**SB1**	Stable Boy One
D	Deer	**SB2**	Stable Boy Two
H	Hunters	**M**	Master

THE DEER IN THE BARN

📖 **Narrator:** A deer was being chased by dogs. Soon the deer saw a barn and ran inside.

D   **Deer:** I can hide in here. I'll just burrow down into this hay where no one can see me.   1

📖 **Narrator:** Soon the hunters came riding up.

H   **Hunters:** Hey, stable boys! Have you seen a deer come by here?   2

SB1   **Stable Boy One:** I just had my dinner, so I have only returned.   3

H   **Hunters:** How about you? Could you look in that barn?   4

SB2   **Stable Boy Two:** I just woke from my midday nap. But I'll look around for you.   5

📖 **Narrator:** The stable boy looked around but didn't see anything. The hunters went away and the deer made his plans to escape.

D   **Deer:** If only I can stay hidden until nightfall. Then I can get away.   6

📖 **Narrator:** But soon after the hunters left, the master came to see if the stable boys were doing their work. He noticed something strange about the hay.

M   **Master:** What is that sticking up in the hay?   7

SB1   **Stable Boy One:** Why, it must be that deer the hunters were looking for.   8

SB2   **Stable Boy Two:** That's right. They thought it might have run in here.   9

M   **Master:** Well, make an end of him. And don't waste any more time.   10

📖 **Narrator:** And so the stable boys killed the deer, who had learned that: *Nothing escapes the master's eye.*

THE DONKEY'S BRAINS

SUMMARY

A fox tells a lion how they can trick the donkey so they can have food for their dinner. After killing the donkey, the lion takes a nap while the fox eats the donkey's brains. When the lion complains to the fox about eating the brains, the fox outwits the lion. (Aesop) *Reading level: 2.*

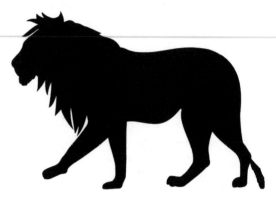

PRESENTATION SUGGESTIONS

The narrator should be off to one side, with the lion and the fox sharing center stage. Consider pairing this fable with "The Lion and the Bull" on page 62 or "The Lion, the Bear, and the Fox" on page 64.

PROPS

The lion and the fox could wear gold and red T-shirts, respectively; have labels; or have simple costumes.

DELIVERY

The lion should sound majestic. The fox should sound clever.

CHARACTERS

📖	Narrator
F	Fox
L	Lion

THE DONKEY'S BRAINS

 Narrator: One day the lion and the fox went hunting together. They didn't find much and became quite hungry.

F   **Fox:** Your Highness, I have an idea for how we can get our dinner.   **1**

L   **Lion:** How is that?   **2**

F   **Fox:** Send a message to the donkey that you want him to be your friend. Then when he comes to meet you, you can kill him. Then we'll share the meal.   **3**

L   **Lion:** That is a great idea. Let's see if it will work.   **4**

      Narrator: The donkey was happy with the invitation and came to meet the lion. When he got there, the lion quickly killed him.

L   **Lion:** Here is our dinner, Master Fox. You watch the donkey while I take a nap. Don't touch him, though, or you will surely suffer.   **5**

      Narrator: The lion went away and took a long nap. The fox got very hungry.

F   **Fox:** I think I'll just have this little snack until the lion returns.   **6**

      Narrator: The fox took out the donkey's brains and ate them up. When the lion came back he saw that the brains were gone.

L   **Lion:** Fox! What have you done with the brains?   **7**

F   **Fox:** Brains, Your Majesty? That donkey had no brains. If he had any brains, he wouldn't have fallen for our trap!   **8**

      Narrator: And once again the fox proved that: *The quick-witted always have an answer ready.*

THE FOX AND THE CAT

SUMMARY

The fox devises a hundred escape plans, but the cat has only one. They soon learn which is better when the hounds arrive. (Aesop)
Reading level: 2.

PRESENTATION SUGGESTIONS

The cat and fox could sit casually on stools or on the ground, looking relaxed as they discuss their escape options. To add interest to this script, consider dressing up the narrator as the tree.

PROPS

The cat and fox could be dressed in black, brown, or reddish-brown simple clothing. The tree could be represented by a mural, or the narrator could play both roles.

DELIVERY

The fox and the cat could sound conversational at first. The fox should sound very indecisive as he tries to decide how to escape the hounds. The cat could sound judgmental at the end.

CHARACTERS

	Narrator
F	Fox
C	Cat

From *Fifty Fabulous Fables*. © 1997 Suzanne I. Barchers. Teacher Ideas Press. (800) 237-6124.

THE FOX AND THE CAT

 Narrator: The fox and the cat were good friends, but on this day the fox was bragging.

F	**Fox:** I have a whole bag of tricks, which contains a hundred ways to escape my enemies.	1
C	**Cat:** I have only one way, but it's usually enough for me.	2
F	**Fox:** Just one way to escape? I'd rather have my bag of tricks than only one way!	3
C	**Cat:** That may be, but I am content with my lot.	4

 Narrator: Just then they heard a pack of hounds coming toward them.

C	**Cat:** Time to use my way to escape. I'll be up in that tree until they leave. What are you going to do to get away from the hounds?	5
F	**Fox:** Let's see. I have so many choices. I need some time to think. I could do this favorite of mine. It's worked before. But they really are sounding too close for that one. Maybe I need this other one.	6

 Narrator: Meanwhile, the hounds came closer and closer. At last the fox was so caught up in deciding what to do that the hounds caught him. The huntsman soon killed him.

C	**Cat:** It's too bad about the fox. He should have listened to me. *Better one safe way than a hundred that you can't count on.*	7

THE FOX AND THE STORK

SUMMARY

In this fable, the fox and the stork are friends. When the fox invites the stork for dinner, he serves soup that only he can lap up. The stork returns the trick at a later date. (Aesop) *Reading level: 2.*

PRESENTATION SUGGESTIONS

Because there are only three characters, consider pairing this script with other fox scripts, or let two or three different sets of students present it to small groups of listeners instead of to the whole class.

PROPS

Consider having various dishes, including a shallow dish and jar, on the side of the stage. This adds to the setting without giving away the story. If the students decide to act out the script more fully, they could add large neckerchiefs or dinner napkins as bibs.

DELIVERY

Most of the delivery should be conversational until each animal realizes there will be no dinner. At the end, the stork should sound judgmental.

CHARACTERS

📖	Narrator
F	Fox
S	Stork

THE FOX AND THE STORK

Narrator: There was a time when the fox and the stork were very good friends. They enjoyed talking about their days. One day they decided to share a meal together.

F   **Fox:** Why don't you come to dinner, my good friend? I'll fix my best soup!   **1**

S   **Stork:** That sounds fine! When shall I come?   **2**

F   **Fox:** Tonight would be good for me.   **3**

Narrator: That night, the stork was happy just thinking about a bowl of good soup. She even arrived a little early at the fox's den.

F   **Fox:** Hello, my friend. Let's waste no time. The soup is ready.   **4**

Narrator: But the stork had quite a surprise. The soup was in a shallow bowl. She couldn't eat any of it with her long beak.

S   **Stork:** My beak is much too long to be able to eat from that bowl, fox.   **5**

F   **Fox:** I *am* sorry that you don't like my soup.   **6**

Narrator: And so the stork went home hungry. But the next day she invited the fox to dinner.

S   **Stork:** Fox, let's forget that I went home hungry last night. Why don't you come to my home for dinner tonight?   **7**

F   **Fox:** It would be my pleasure.   **8**

Narrator: That night the fox showed up at the stork's home, eager for another meal.

S   **Stork:**   Welcome, welcome, dear friend. I knew you liked soup,   9
so I made *my* favorite for our meal.

F   **Fox:**   I have looked forward to this all day, my friend.   10

Narrator: When the stork served the soup, the fox found that
he was in for a surprise. The soup was served in a long-necked
jar with a narrow top.

F   **Fox:**   What have you done? I can't get even my snout in this jar!   11

S   **Stork:**   I *am* sorry that you don't like my soup. Perhaps you would   12
like to lick the outside of the jar when I am done.

Narrator: And so the stork ate all her dinner, leaving the fox with
very little in his stomach.

S   **Stork:**   Good night, dear fox. Next time you invite me to dinner,   13
just remember: *One bad turn deserves another.*

From *Fifty Fabulous Fables.* © 1997 Suzanne I. Barchers. Teacher Ideas Press. (800) 237-6124.

THE FOX WITHOUT A TAIL

SUMMARY

When a fox loses his tail, he tries to convince the other foxes to get rid of theirs also. (Aesop)
Reading level: 2.

PRESENTATION SUGGESTIONS

The fox could begin onstage with the narrator. The other foxes could come onstage and sit on the floor, turned sideways as if listening to the fox, so the audience can see all the characters. Add various foxes in the group as non-speaking roles, if desired. This fable could be paired with other fables about foxes.

PROPS

Students could wear brown T-shirts. All could have felt tails attached, except for the first fox.

DELIVERY

The fox without a tail should sound persuasive. Foxes two through four should sound like they are becoming convinced that the fox without the tail may be right. The older fox should sound wise.

CHARACTERS

📖	Narrator
F1	Fox One
F2	Fox Two
F3	Fox Three
F4	Fox Four
OF	Old Fox

THE FOX WITHOUT A TAIL

Narrator: A fox caught his tail in a trap. He struggled to get free. But instead, he lost all of his tail except for the stump.

F1   **Fox One:**   This is terrible. I can't face the other foxes with no tail! I have to think of a plan.   **1**

Narrator: The fox thought for a while. Then he called together all the other foxes for a meeting.

F1   **Fox One:**   Thank you for coming today. I have something important to share with you.   **2**

F2   **Fox Two:**   What is it, brother?   **3**

F1   **Fox One:**   Have you noticed how the dogs can catch you by the tail?   **4**

F3   **Fox Three:**   That nearly happened to me, but I got away just in time.   **5**

F1   **Fox One:**   Have you noticed that when we want to sit down and have a conversation, our tails get in the way?   **6**

F4   **Fox Four:**   Now that you mention it, I guess our tails do get in the way a bit.   **7**

F1   **Fox One:**   Now you know why I have gotten rid of mine. There really is no use for keeping a tail. I suggest you all get rid of yours.   **8**

OF   **Old Fox:**   You may have lost your tail. But would you have suggested this if you still had yours? After all, our tails are quite beautiful.   **9**

Narrator: And so the other foxes realized that their brother was looking out only for himself, and they all kept their tails. *A wise fox looks out for himself.*

THE GOOSE THAT LAID
THE GOLDEN EGGS

SUMMARY

A farmer's goose begins to lay golden eggs. The farmer and his wife enjoy their new wealth until the farmer decides to open the goose to find all the eggs inside. (Aesop)
Reading level: 2.

PRESENTATION SUGGESTIONS

The farmer and his wife should share center stage, perhaps talking directly to each other, rather than to the audience. This fable provides opportunities for students to practice different facial expressions, as they show astonishment over the eggs and finally despair over their loss. Consider pairing this fable with "Greed and Envy" on page 94.

PROPS

The farmer and his wife could be dressed poorly at the beginning of the play. They could don fine hats, scarves, or other nearby props as the eggs are sold.

DELIVERY

This script gives several opportunities for particularly effective vocal expression. The farmer and his wife should sound amazed at the discovery of the golden eggs and gleeful at their newfound wealth.

CHARACTERS

   📖   Narrator

F   Farmer

W   Wife

THE GOOSE THAT LAID THE GOLDEN EGGS

Narrator: There once was a farmer who lived happily with his wife. They didn't have much, but they did have a fine goose. And every day this fine goose laid an egg so big that they could each eat a hearty breakfast. Each day the farmer would go to the shed and collect the egg. Then his wife would cook their breakfast. But one day he found a surprise.

F   **Farmer:**   What is this? Where is my goose egg? This egg is yellow and way too heavy to be anything that we can eat. I had better get my wife so we can decide what to do.   **1**

Narrator: The farmer brought his wife out to the shed.

F   **Farmer:**   Look at this egg, wife! It's useless. What will we eat for our breakfast?   **2**

W   **Wife:**   Wait a minute, husband. Look closely at that egg. I think it is made of gold.   **3**

F   **Farmer:**   Gold! That couldn't be. Someone has played a trick on us.   **4**

W   **Wife:**   Don't be so sure. Let's take it to town and find out what it is.   **5**

Narrator: So the farmer and his wife took the egg to town and learned that it was truly pure gold.

W   **Wife:**   Well, husband, what are we going to do with this egg of gold?   **6**

F   **Farmer:**   First we're going to sell it, my dear! Then we will buy the finest breakfast we've ever had. And, finally, we will shop for whatever suits your heart's desire.   **7**

From *Fifty Fabulous Fables*. © 1997 Suzanne I. Barchers. Teacher Ideas Press. (800) 237-6124.

📖 **Narrator:**   And so the farmer and his wife had a wonderful day of shopping in the town. The next day they both went out to the shed together and tiptoed up to the goose. They peeked inside the nest.

F &
W   **Farmer and Wife:**   Ahh! Another golden egg!   8

📖 **Narrator:**   The farmer and wife danced a jig of delight. Then they took that egg into the town and enjoyed selling it and buying themselves new things. Every day this happened, and the couple became quite rich. But one day the farmer became very greedy.

F   **Farmer:**   Wife, I am going to open the goose to find all the gold inside.   9

W   **Wife:**   No, husband. If you do that, you will kill the goose for sure.   10

F   **Farmer:**   But we have to wait a day for the next egg. This takes too long. There are too many things that I want to buy.   11

📖 **Narrator:**   In spite of his wife's pleading, the farmer picked up his ax and opened the goose with one stroke. Inside he found nothing. To his sadness, he learned that: *One shouldn't kill the goose that lays the golden eggs.*

From *Fifty Fabulous Fables*. © 1997 Suzanne I. Barchers. Teacher Ideas Press. (800) 237-6124.

THE LION AND THE BULL

SUMMARY

A lion tricks a bull into coming to his house for a feast. The bull realizes that he is the intended feast and leaves. (Aesop)
Reading level: 2.

PRESENTATION SUGGESTIONS

The narrator should stand to the side, with the lion in the center and the bull on the other side. Consider pairing this fable with "The Donkey's Brains" on page 50 or "The Lion, the Bear, and the Fox" on page 64.

PROPS

The lion could wear a gold T-shirt and sit in front of boxes painted to look like rocks. The bull could be dressed in black.

DELIVERY

Both the lion and the bull should sound strong and forceful. The lion should sound frustrated at the end when the bull leaves.

CHARACTERS

📖	Narrator
L	Lion
B	Bull

THE LION AND THE BULL

Narrator: A hungry lion hoped to capture a large bull so that he could have many fine meals. He knew that he would have to think of a clever way to trick the bull.

Lion: I know what I'll do. I'll send word to the bull that I have caught a fine, fat lamb. I'll ask him to enjoy the feast with me. Once he has come to my table I'll pounce on him and kill him.   1

Narrator: The lion sent the invitation to the bull, who thought feasting on a lamb sounded like a fine dinner.

Bull: I'll send word to the lion that I would like to join him. It should be a good meal.   2

Narrator: The bull arrived at the lion's den. Before greeting the lion, he looked around at the preparations.

Bull: This is quite interesting. Look at all the cooking pots and pans.   3
And why is there such a huge spit over the cooking fire? This looks like the lion has intended to roast someone far larger than a small lamb.

Narrator: Just then the lion saw the bull.

Lion: Welcome, my friend. Come in, come in. Have a seat at my table.   4

Bull: Sorry, but I'll not come in for *this* feast.   5

Lion: Why not? I haven't done anything to harm you. You have no   6
reason to leave. Please don't go.

Bull: I have seen enough to give me reason. This looks like you have   7
prepared to cook a very large bull rather than a very plump lamb. You'll have to find another bull for your feast.

Narrator: And so the lion learned that: *You can't trick everyone.*

THE LION, THE BEAR, AND THE FOX

SUMMARY

A hungry lion and bear kill a fawn together. An argument over who will get to eat the fawn exhausts them, and a fox takes the fawn home for his family. (Aesop)
Reading level: 2.

PRESENTATION SUGGESTIONS

The narrator should stand to one side, with the lion and the bear in the center. The fox should enter for his part and exit triumphantly at the end of the play. This fable could be paired with "The Donkey's Brains" on page 50 or "The Lion and the Bull" on page 62.

PROPS

Consider dressing the characters in brown, gold, black, or reddish-brown T-shirts or with tails that match their roles.

DELIVERY

The lion and the bear should sound conversational at first, then argumentative, and finally weak. The fox should sound delighted at his good fortune.

CHARACTERS

	Narrator
L	Lion
B	Bear
F	Fox

THE LION, THE BEAR, AND THE FOX

  **Narrator:** A hungry lion and bear were prowling the forest.

L **Lion:** I am so hungry. I haven't had a meal for days! 1

B **Bear:** Me too, my friend. What I wouldn't give for a big supper right now! 2

Narrator: Just then they came upon a small fawn who hadn't seen them. Both of the mighty beasts gave a swipe of their strong paws, and the fawn quickly died.

L **Lion:** This is my meal! I killed her with my mighty claws. 3

B **Bear:** Not so, my friend! I hit her the hardest with my wicked paw. 4

L **Lion:** You'll not get this meal from me. I have been too hungry for too many days! 5

B **Bear:** Just listen to my stomach rumble! That fawn is mine! 6

Narrator: The bear and the lion began to fight over the fawn. Already weakened by hunger, they fought and fought until neither could rise from the ground. Suddenly a fox came along and saw the lion, the bear, and the fawn lying on the ground.

F **Fox:** Aha! Looks like dinner is here for my family and me! 7

Narrator: The fox, who wasn't at all tired, grabbed the small fawn by two legs and began to drag her away. The bear and the lion were too tired even to get up.

L   **Lion:**   Wait, that's our kill!   **8**

B   **Bear:**   That's right! We need our dinner.   **9**

F   **Fox:**   Too bad that you couldn't have worked it out between you. Your loss is my gain.   **10**

Narrator: And with that, the fox took his dinner home to his happy family. The lion and bear learned: *Hungry partners should work together.*

THE MAN AND THE SNAKE

SUMMARY

When a snake bites a boy, the father seeks his revenge. The snake teaches the man that some things are impossible to forgive and forget. (Aesop)

Reading level: 2.

PRESENTATION SUGGESTIONS

The narrator should be positioned off to one side. The boy should leave the stage after his lines. The man and the snake should be in center stage.

PROPS

An "ax" and other farm implements could be on the stage. The father could be dressed like a farmer. The snake could wearing a scarf with a pattern like that of a snakeskin.

DELIVERY

The boy should sound panicked. The man should sound angry and later pleading. The snake should sound sneaky and haughty.

CHARACTERS

📖	Narrator
B	Boy
M	Man
S	Snake

THE MAN AND THE SNAKE

Narrator: A boy was in the yard with his father. He happened to step on a snake's tail. The snake coiled up and bit him.

B   **Boy:**   Father! Something just bit me!   **1**

Narrator: Sad to say, the boy died from the snakebite. The father was full of anger and grief.

M   **Man:**   I am going to have my revenge on that snake. I am going to get my ax and kill it.   **2**

Narrator: The man chased the snake around his yard and cut off part of its tail.

S   **Snake:**   Ssss. You'll be sorry you did that! Just wait, my friend.   **3**

Narrator: In turn, the snake began biting the man's cattle. After several cattle died, the man decided he had to do something about the snake.

M   **Man:**   Things are only getting worse with the loss of my cattle. I think it is time I made up with that snake.   **4**

Narrator: The man went to the snake to plead with it to stop. He took along gifts of food and honey to the snake's den.

M   **Man:**   Let's forgive and forget. My son shouldn't have stepped on you. And I shouldn't have cut off your tail. But now you have had your revenge on my cattle. Now that we are both satisfied, can't we be friends again?   **5**

S   **Snake:**   No, no. Take away your gifts. You can never forget the loss of your son. And I can't forget the loss of my tail.   **6**

Narrator: Thus, dear listeners, we learn that: *Injuries may be forgiven, but not forgotten.*

From *Fifty Fabulous Fables.* © 1997 Suzanne I. Barchers. Teacher Ideas Press. (800) 237-6124.

THE OLD WOMAN AND THE DOCTOR

SUMMARY

A doctor robs an old woman while he is treating her for problems with her eyes. When he takes her to court to get payment for the treatment, she turns the tables on him. (Aesop) *Reading level: 2.*

PRESENTATION SUGGESTIONS

The narrator should be off to one side, with the woman and doctor in the center. The judge could be in a chair on the other side. The woman and the doctor could move to the judge's side for the final part of the script.

PROPS

The woman could be dressed in a shawl, long dress, and glasses. The doctor could have medical equipment or a black bag. The judge could have a gavel and sit behind a table.

DELIVERY

The old woman should sound old and frail. The doctor should sound self-assured. The judge should sound authoritative.

CHARACTERS

📖	Narrator
OW	Old Woman
D	Doctor
J	Judge

THE OLD WOMAN AND THE DOCTOR

Narrator: An old woman was having trouble with her eyes. She sent for the doctor.

OW	**Old Woman:** Doctor, I hope you can fix these eyes of mine. It is getting very hard to see.	1
D	**Doctor:** I'll have you seeing in no time. But can you pay me five coins for curing you?	2
OW	**Old Woman:** That sounds fair. If I am cured, I'll happily pay you.	3
D	**Doctor:** Fine, then. Let me put this ointment on your eyes. But it's really important that you keep your eyes closed until after I have left.	4
OW	**Old Woman:** Thank you, sir. I'll just rest my eyes for a bit. You can let yourself out the door.	5

Narrator: While she rested her eyes, the doctor carried off a piece of furniture from her house. This happened during every appointment. The old woman closed her eyes and the doctor stole something from her home. Finally, the old woman had little left. The doctor presented her with the bill.

D	**Doctor:** Well, I do believe you are cured. It's time for you to pay me.	6
OW	**Old Woman:** I'll not pay you one coin!	7
D	**Doctor:** Then I'll have to take you to court.	8

Narrator: And the doctor did just that.

J	**Judge:** Well, tell me what this is all about.	9

D   **Doctor:**   This woman promised me five coins if I cured her eyes.   **10**
I treated her many times and now she is cured. Yet she won't pay me.

J   **Judge:**   Well, old woman, how do you answer this?   **11**

OW   **Old Woman:**   It's true he treated me many times, but he has not   **12**
cured me.

J   **Judge:**   How is that?   **13**

OW   **Old Woman:**   Before his cures, I could at least see the furniture in   **14**
my house. Now I can't even see that!

Narrator: And so the doctor learned that: *One can't trick someone twice.*

THE THIEF AND HIS MOTHER

SUMMARY

A boy steals repeatedly, and his mother encourages him. When he is sentenced to death, he blames his mother for not having punished him for his thefts. (Aesop)
Reading level: 2.

PRESENTATION SUGGESTIONS

The thief and his mother should have center stage, with the narrator to one side. Several students could play the role of the friends at the beginning of the play.

PROPS

The thief could have a pack with a rubber chicken, notebooks, and coat hanging out of it. The mother could wear a long dress and shawl.

DELIVERY

At first, the mother and thief should sound proud of his thefts. The judge should sound authoritative and decisive. The thief should sound angry at the end.

CHARACTERS

📖	Narrator
F	Friends
M	Mother
T	Thief
J	Judge

THE THIEF AND HIS MOTHER

 Narrator: A boy stole some notebooks from his friends at school. His friends brought him to his mother to be punished.

F	**Friends:** Your son stole our notebooks. What are you going to do?	1
M	**Mother:** My son must be clever. Maybe you should take better care of your things.	2
	Narrator: Next the boy stole a chicken for their dinner.	
T	**Thief:** Mother, look what I brought you.	3
M	**Mother:** Aha! Very good, my son. We'll make a fine meal of that chicken.	4
	Narrator: Next the boy stole a coat.	
T	**Thief:** Mother, look what I brought you.	5
M	**Mother:** You are so quick and clever. I'll look good in that fine coat.	6
	Narrator: The boy's stealing went on for many years. He got bigger, and he stole more. Finally, he was caught and taken to the judge.	
J	**Judge:** Everyone knows that you have stolen from the people for many years. I hereby sentence you to death.	7
	Narrator: The day came for him to be put to death. His mother walked beside him, crying hard.	
T	**Thief:** May I say something to my mother before I die?	8
J	**Judge:** Of course.	9
	Narrator: His mother leaned close to hear what he had to say. The thief bit her hard on the ear. The mother cried with pain.	
J	**Judge:** First you steal and now you hurt your mother! Why did you do that?	10
T	**Thief:** If only she had punished me when I first began to steal. Then I would not be dying today. *Punishment always finds a victim.*	11

THE TORTOISE AND THE BIRDS

SUMMARY

The eagle is giving the tortoise a ride to a new home when the crow convinces the eagle that the tortoise would make a fine meal for them. (Aesop)
Reading level: 2.

PRESENTATION SUGGESTIONS

Have the tortoise stand near the middle of the stage, with the narrator on one side and the eagle and the crow on the other.

PROPS

Consider having a backdrop that shows the sea, rocks, and clouds. The characters could be dressed in gray, brown, or black T-shirts.

DELIVERY

The delivery should be conversational between the eagle and the tortoise. The crow should sound wheedling.

CHARACTERS

📖	Narrator
T	Tortoise
E	Eagle
C	Crow

THE TORTOISE AND THE BIRDS

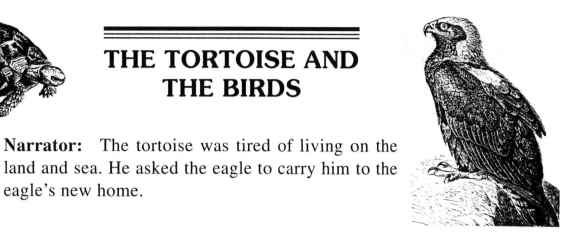

Narrator: The tortoise was tired of living on the land and sea. He asked the eagle to carry him to the eagle's new home.

T	**Tortoise:** Eagle, will you carry me to your new home? I promise you a fine reward for your trouble.	1
E	**Eagle:** Of course, my friend. Let me grab you with my strong talons and off we'll go.	2
	Narrator: On the way they met a crow.	
C	**Crow:** Eagle, don't you know that a tortoise is good eating?	3
E	**Eagle:** The shell is so hard that we couldn't get at the meat.	4
C	**Crow:** But you could drop the tortoise on the rocks. The shell will crack on the rocks, and we'll have a fine meal.	5
E	**Eagle:** You're right, crow. But tortoise promised me a fine reward for taking him to my new home.	6
C	**Crow:** Did he tell you what that reward would be?	7
E	**Eagle:** Now that you mention it, he didn't.	8
T	**Tortoise:** But eagle, I promised you a reward, and you shall have it!	9
C	**Crow:** What better reward than giving us a fine meal?	10

Narrator: With that, the eagle dropped the tortoise on the rock. His shell cracked, and the eagle and the crow made a fine meal of him. *Sometimes the reward is unexpected.*

From *Fifty Fabulous Fables*. © 1997 Suzanne I. Barchers. Teacher Ideas Press. (800) 237-6124.

THE WOLF AND THE LAMB

SUMMARY

A wolf seizes upon any excuse to eat a young lamb in this tale that rationalizes the behavior of bullies. (Aesop)

Reading level: 2.

PRESENTATION SUGGESTIONS

Consider pairing this fable with one in which the wolf does not succeed, such as "The Wolf, the Mother, and the Child" on page 78. Challenge the students to also rewrite the ending of this fable so that the wolf fails. Because acting out the existing ending could be considered offensive, have the students do a formal reading of the tale instead.

PROPS

Simple props that indicate the outdoor setting would enhance the story.

DELIVERY

The wolf should sound sneaky and bullying. The lamb should sound meek and pleading.

CHARACTERS

📖	Narrator
W	Wolf
L	Lamb

From *Fifty Fabulous Fables*. © 1997 Suzanne I. Barchers. Teacher Ideas Press. (800) 237-6124.

THE WOLF AND THE LAMB

Narrator: Once upon a time a wolf lapped up water at a river. After filling his belly, he saw a lamb drinking just downstream.

W   **Wolf:** Aha! There's my dinner! All I have to do is think of an excuse for eating it. Let's see.   1

Narrator: The wolf thought for a moment. It didn't take him long to make up an excuse.

W   **Wolf:** How dare you muddy the water I'm drinking!   3

L   **Lamb:** No, no. I can't be making your water muddy. I'm drinking *down* the river from you. Your water runs *down* to me.   4

Narrator: The wolf thought up another excuse.

W   **Wolf:** But a year ago you called me bad names. Why did you do that?   5

L   **Lamb:** That couldn't have been me. I am only six months old.   6

Narrator: The wolf thought again.

W   **Wolf:** Then that must have been your father.   7

Narrator: And the wolf grabbed the lamb and ate her up. But before she died she bleated: *A bully uses any excuse.*

THE WOLF, THE MOTHER, AND THE CHILD

SUMMARY

A wolf lurks in hiding outside a village, hoping for a meal. When a mother threatens her crying child with feeding him to the wolf, the wolf thinks he has found a meal. (La Fontaine and Aesop) *Reading level: 2.*

PRESENTATION SUGGESTIONS

The mother and child could have center stage, with the wolf lurking to one side and the narrator on the other side. Nonspeaking roles could be held by the various animals mentioned by the narrator: lamb, calf, turkey, chicken. Those children could have simple costumes and emerge from a designated backstage or screened area, making the appropriate animal sounds as they enter and leave the stage.

PROPS

The mother could wear an apron and shawl and carry a doll in one arm. The wolf could wear a large bib, as if he were preparing for dinner. A mural or backdrop could indicate the house.

DELIVERY

The wolf should sound gruff until he is caught. Then he should sound whiny and ingratiating. The mother should sound exasperated at her child and then outraged at the wolf's intentions.

CHARACTERS

📖	Narrator	CA	Calves (nonspeaking, optional)
W	Wolf	T	Turkeys (nonspeaking, optional)
M	Mother	CH	Chickens (nonspeaking, optional)
L	Lambs (nonspeaking, optional)		

THE WOLF, THE MOTHER, AND THE CHILD

Narrator: Wolves are always hungry, and the wolf in our story is *very* hungry. He is waiting outside a mother's home, listening to her child cry, and hoping for dinner. Let's see what happens.

W   **Wolf:** Grrr. It's been too long since I have eaten a good meal. Here comes a lamb! But if I kill it, it will bleat and someone will hear it!   **1**

   Narrator: The wolf let the lamb go on. Soon a calf walked by the wolf.

W   **Wolf:** Here comes a calf! But if I kill it, it will moo and someone will hear it!   **2**

   Narrator: The wolf let the calf go on. Soon a turkey walked by the wolf.

W   **Wolf:** Here comes a turkey! But if I kill it, it will gobble and someone will hear it!   **3**

   Narrator: The wolf let the turkey go on. Soon a chicken walked by the wolf.

W   **Wolf:** Here comes a chicken! But if I kill it, it will cackle and someone will hear it!   **4**

   Narrator: Just then the wolf heard the mother inside the house.

M   **Mother:** Child, you must stop crying. If you don't stop, I am going to feed you to the next wolf I see.   **5**

   Narrator: When the child didn't stop crying, the wolf became very excited.

From *Fifty Fabulous Fables*. © 1997 Suzanne I. Barchers. Teacher Ideas Press. (800) 237-6124.

W   **Wolf:**   Ah! My luck has turned! Eating this child will stop the   **6**
noise, and the mother will be happy! It is time to show myself so
she can feed me my dinner!

Narrator: The mother looked out the window. Seeing the wolf,
she called to her dog.

M   **Mother:**   Dog! There is a wolf outside our door! Chase it off before   **7**
I have to kill it.

Narrator: Just then the dog burst from the house and grabbed the
wolf by the neck. The mother followed the dog outside.

M   **Mother:**   What are you doing here, you great beast?   **8**

W   **Wolf:**   What is this? How can you treat me like this? I haven't had a   **9**
meal in days. And I heard you say you were going to feed your boy to
the next wolf you saw.

M   **Mother:**   Did you think I would give my boy to you? He will never   **10**
fill your belly, no matter how much he cries.

Narrator: And with that, she grabbed a nearby pitchfork and killed
the wolf. After cutting off his right front paw, she nailed it to her door
to remind other wolves: *Never try to eat a mother's child.*

From *Fifty Fabulous Fables.* © 1997 Suzanne I. Barchers. Teacher Ideas Press. (800) 237-6124.

PART 3

THE BOY WHO CRIED WOLF

SUMMARY

A boy tending his flock of sheep decides to cause some excitement by alerting the villagers to a nonexistent wolf. When a wolf really appears, the villagers will no longer come to his aid. (Aesop)
Reading level: 3.

PRESENTATION SUGGESTIONS

The narrator should stand on one side of the stage, with the boy next to him or her. The villagers could enter from the other side and leave after each response to the boy's cries.

PROPS

The boy could hold a shepherd's crook and wear a simple cap. The villagers (both male and female) could be dressed in workers' clothes, perhaps portraying various trades (blacksmith, baker, cook, and so forth).

DELIVERY

The boy should sound especially frantic the last time he calls for help. The villagers should sound annoyed with him at the end of the script.

CHARACTERS

📖	Narrator
B	Boy
V1	Villager One
V2	Villager Two
V3	Villager Three

THE BOY WHO CRIED WOLF

Narrator: Once a young boy tended sheep at the foot of a mountain near a dark forest. He was a good boy, but he got lonely on that mountain. One day, he thought of a plan so that he could have a bit of company and a little excitement.

B   **Boy:** I know what I'll do! I'll run toward the village raising the alarm that a wolf is after the sheep. People will come up to help. The wolf will be gone, but I'll have some fun on this boring day.   **1**

Narrator: So the boy ran toward the village.

B   **Boy:** Help! Help! Wolf! Wolf!   **2**

Narrator: Several of the villagers came running to meet him. They ran to the flock of sheep but decided the wolf must have run off.

V1   **Villager One:** The wolf must be gone. We'll go back to work, but take care, now.   **3**

V2   **Villager Two:** And call us if another wolf comes.   **4**

V3   **Villager Three:** We don't want you to lose any sheep!   **5**

Narrator: A few days later the boy got bored again. He decided to try the same trick and ran toward the village.

B   **Boy:** Help! Help! Wolf! Wolf!   **6**

Narrator: Again, several of the villagers came running to meet him. They ran to the flock of sheep but again decided the wolf must have run off.

V1   **Villager One:** Well, you are lucky again.   **7**

| V2 | **Villager Two:**   But how could a wolf get away so quickly? | **8** |

| V3 | **Villager Three:**   Be watchful, son, but be sure there really is a wolf. We are busy people, you know. | **9** |

Narrator: The villagers returned to their work, but shortly after this a real wolf did come out of the forest. It began to stalk the sheep, and the boy couldn't chase it off. The boy ran toward the village.

| B | **Boy:**   Help! Help! Wolf! Wolf! | **10** |

| V1 | **Villager One:**   I am tired of that boy calling out when there is no wolf. | **11** |

| V2 | **Villager Two:**   Does he think we are stupid? | **12** |

| V3 | **Villager Three:**   I'm not going to be made a fool of again. I'm staying right here. | **13** |

Narrator: And so the wolf had a good meal with the boy's flock. The boy learned too late that: *A liar will not be believed, even when he speaks the truth.*

From *Fifty Fabulous Fables*. © 1997 Suzanne I. Barchers. Teacher Ideas Press. (800) 237-6124.

THE DEER AND THE HUNTER

SUMMARY

A deer admires his antlers and dislikes his slim legs. He learns all too late that he should have appreciated his legs. (Aesop)

Reading level: 3.

PRESENTATION SUGGESTIONS

The narrator should stand on one side, with the deer in the middle and the hunter on the other side.

PROPS

A mural could show a tree, pond, and other forest features. A set of bow and arrows could be propped on stage or over the hunter's shoulder. The deer could be dressed in brown clothing, and the hunter could have a red vest and cap.

DELIVERY

The deer should sound boastful or proud. The hunter should sound eager to make the kill.

CHARACTERS

    📖   Narrator

D   Deer

H   Hunter

THE DEER AND THE HUNTER

 Narrator: A deer was drinking from a pond, admiring how he looked.

D   **Deer:** What fine antlers I have! They make a crown on my head. It's too bad my legs are so slim. Bigger legs would be better able to carry my antlers.   **1**

 Narrator: Just then a hunter came along.

H   **Hunter:** Aha! At last I have found my dinner!   **2**

 Narrator: As the hunter placed an arrow in his bow, the deer spotted him. The deer bounded away on his slim legs with the arrow whistling nearby. The deer was nearly away, but he wasn't looking at where he was going.

H   **Hunter:** Lucky for me! That deer has caught its antlers in those low tree branches. Now I can easily kill it.   **3**

 Narrator: As the hunter came close, the deer knew that he should have been happy to have his slim but fast legs.

D   **Deer:** Now I have learned a sad lesson: *What we often dislike is what is most useful to us.*   **4**

From *Fifty Fabulous Fables.* © 1997 Suzanne I. Barchers. Teacher Ideas Press. (800) 237-6124.

THE FOUR OXEN AND THE LION

SUMMARY

Four oxen work together to stay safe from the lion. After a quarrel they separate and become vulnerable to the lion's attack. (Aesop)
Reading level: 3.

PRESENTATION SUGGESTIONS

The narrator should stand on one side, with the four oxen arranged in order from the middle to one side. After their quarrel they could move to four different areas of the stage.

PROPS

The oxen could be labeled "one" through "four" or simply be dressed in dark colors. The stage could have four areas indicated by four chairs.

DELIVERY

The oxen should sound conversational and then argumentative.

CHARACTERS

📖	Narrator
O1	Ox One
O2	Ox Two
O3	Ox Three
O4	Ox Four
LI	Lion (nonspeaking, optional)

THE FOUR OXEN AND THE LION

Narrator: Four oxen lived together in a field. They were quite happy except for their fear of a lion that lived nearby. It often lurked about, and the oxen were afraid that someday it would get hungry enough to attack.

| O1 | **Ox One:** Someday that lion is going to attack. We need to have a plan. | 1 |

| O2 | **Ox Two:** I agree with you, brother. Somehow we must decide how to use our horns. They are our strongest weapons. | 2 |

| O3 | **Ox Three:** I have an idea. Whenever the lion comes near, let us put our tails toward each other. | 3 |

| O4 | **Ox Four:** Good idea, brother. Then the lion will be facing all our horns! We should be quite safe then. | 4 |

Narrator: Many times the lion tried to attack the oxen. But each time they turned their tails toward each other with their heads turned out. The lion couldn't fight against their horns and always retreated.

| O1 | **Ox One:** Our plan to defeat the lion seems to be working. I am glad we thought of it. | 5 |

| O2 | **Ox Two:** *We* thought of it? I don't remember your having any good ideas. | 6 |

| O3 | **Ox Three:** You must admit that neither of you were much help. | 7 |

| O4 | **Ox Four:** That's right, it was my fine brother and I who made the plan work. | 8 |

Narrator: The four oxen continued to argue and decided they would no longer work together. Each went off to a corner of the field. The lion, seeing this new development, went to each corner of the field also and attacked them one by one. Soon all four were dead. So don't forget, dear listeners, the lesson in this story: *United we stand; divided we fall.*

From *Fifty Fabulous Fables*. © 1997 Suzanne I. Barchers. Teacher Ideas Press. (800) 237-6124.

THE FOX AND THE MOSQUITOES

SUMMARY

When a fox gets stuck in a bush, mosquitoes feast on his tail. The hedgehog tries to help, but the fox declines. (Aesop)
Reading level: 3.

PRESENTATION SUGGESTIONS

This short fable could begin with the narrator and the fox onstage. The hedgehog could come in just for its lines. This tale offers students an opportunity to continue the story past the ending Aesop provides. Students could predict what happens next and write several episodes, perhaps ending with an animal helping the fox to get untangled.

PROPS

The fox could be in a red or russet T-shirt, with the hedgehog in beige or brown. A large plant could serve as the bush.

DELIVERY

The fox should sound frustrated by his situation. The hedgehog should sound helpful.

CHARACTERS

📖	Narrator
F	Fox
H	Hedgehog

THE FOX AND THE MOSQUITOES

 Narrator: A fox crossed a river and got his tail caught in a bush.

F   **Fox:** What bad luck! I seem to be stuck fast. These bushes are too prickly.   **1**

 Narrator: A number of mosquitoes saw that the fox was stuck. They flew closer and decided to stay for a meal.

F   **Fox:** Those pesky mosquitoes! They are sure enjoying my blood.   **2**

 Narrator: Just then a hedgehog came by.

H   **Hedgehog:** Mr. Fox, it looks like you are in a bit of trouble.   **3**

F   **Fox:** Yes, I am quite stuck here.   **4**

H   **Hedgehog:** Would you like me to get rid of those mosquitoes who are sucking your blood?   **5**

F   **Fox:** Thank you, Mr. Hedgehog, but I would rather you didn't.   **6**

H   **Hedgehog:** Why not?   **7**

F   **Fox:** Well, these mosquitoes have nearly had their fill. If you drive them away, others will come. They will be hungry and will bleed me to death!   **8**

H   **Hedgehog:** As you wish, Mr. Fox. Good day!   **9**

 Narrator: No one knows if the fox got untangled from the bush. But at least no more mosquitoes got to feast on him that day! *One problem could be worse than another.*

THE FOX, THE ROOSTER, AND THE DOG

SUMMARY

When a fox tries to trick a rooster by telling him all the beasts will be living together peacefully, the rooster outwits the fox. (Aesop)
Reading level: 3.

PRESENTATION SUGGESTIONS

The narrator could stand off to the side, with the fox prowling around the stage until he spots the rooster. Place the rooster on a stool so he is higher than the fox.

PROPS

Consider using simple costumes for the two animals. The fox could be dressed in a brown T-shirt, and the rooster could have a red comb or feathers.

DELIVERY

The fox should sound convincing and sly. The rooster should sound sincere and self-assured.

CHARACTERS

📖	Narrator
F	Fox
R	Rooster

THE FOX, THE ROOSTER, AND THE DOG

Narrator: One night the moon was shining brightly. A fox prowled around a farmer's yard, hoping to find something to eat. Soon the fox saw a rooster high on the henhouse.

F	**Fox:** Say, my friend! I have good news for you!	1

F **Fox:** Say, my friend! I have good news for you! **1**

R **Rooster:** I doubt that you have any news for me, but go ahead and tell me what you have to say. **2**

F **Fox:** King Lion has declared a truce. No beast may hurt another any more, and everyone is going to live together in friendship! **3**

R **Rooster:** That is good news! And here comes someone who will be happy to hear all about this. **4**

Narrator: The rooster stretched his neck and looked off toward the farmer's house.

F **Fox:** What do you see? **5**

R **Rooster:** I see my master's dog coming. He will be happy with your news! **6**

Narrator: The fox began to leave in a hurry.

R **Rooster:** Going so soon? Don't you want to stop and tell my master's dog about the good news? **7**

F **Fox:** I would gladly do that, but I fear he may not have heard about King Lion's decree. **8**

Narrator: And that is how fox learned that: *Sometimes one is just too smart for oneself.*

GREED AND ENVY

SUMMARY

When two neighbors, one greedy and one envious, pray to Jupiter to have their wishes granted, Jupiter teaches them a lesson. (Aesop)
Reading level: 3.

PRESENTATION SUGGESTIONS

This fable has a formal style to it. The narrator and Jupiter should stand on either side of the stage, with the two neighbors dominating center stage. Consider pairing this fable with "The Goose That Laid the Golden Eggs" on page 59.

PROPS

Jupiter could wield a scepter. The two neighbors could wear clothing with some touches that indicate affluence, such as a plumed hat, vest, or leather gloves.

DELIVERY

The neighbors should sound greedy and envious, as appropriate. Jupiter should sound godlike.

CHARACTERS

📖	Narrator
N1	Neighbor One
N2	Neighbor Two
J	Jupiter

GREED AND ENVY

Narrator: Once there were two neighbors who considered themselves wonderful friends until one fateful day. On that day they set out together to pray to Jupiter.

N1	**Neighbor One:** What will you pray for, my friend? You have all that you could possibly need. You have a home that is the envy of all in the village, including me. Your children are well behaved and good citizens. And everyone knows that your wife keeps the finest house in the village.	**1**
N2	**Neighbor Two:** Perhaps you are right, but I can't stop thinking about the homes I saw in the city. Now *that* is where people really know how to live in luxury. I would be perfectly happy if I could see myself in a home worthy of the envy of the city folk.	**2**

Narrator: Jupiter heard their prayers and decided to punish each of them for their greed and envy.

J	**Jupiter:** I will grant you one wish each, but only on one condition. That condition is that whatever one man asks for will be doubled for your neighbor. Is that agreeable?	**3**
N1	**Neighbor One:** That seems fair. After all, we are great friends.	**4**
N2	**Neighbor Two:** I agree. Let's go home to make our wishes.	**5**

Narrator: Upon arriving home, the greedy man and the envious man made their wishes.

N2	**Neighbor Two:** I'll go first. I wish for a room full of gold. Then I can build a finer house than those in the city. I can't wait to see it.	**6**

From *Fifty Fabulous Fables.* © 1997 Suzanne I. Barchers. Teacher Ideas Press. (800) 237-6124.

Narrator: The greedy man was granted his wish, and at the same time the envious man had two rooms of gold. However, he couldn't bear to think of his neighbor having even one room of gold. After all, his neighbor already had so much.

N1   **Neighbor One:**   Why did you wish for a room of gold? You already   7
had so much to begin with! I'll fix you. I wish that *I* would have one of my eyes put out.

Narrator: And with that the envious neighbor lost one of his eyes. But the greedy neighbor lost both his eyes, proving that: *Greed and envy are their own punishment.*

THE HORSE, THE HUNTER, AND THE STAG

SUMMARY

When the horse asks the hunter to help him take revenge on the stag, he falls under the control of the hunter. (Aesop)
Reading level: 3.

PRESENTATION SUGGESTIONS

This story, although short, has a more difficult theme and should lead to good discussions. The horse should be in center stage with the narrator and hunter on either side. The stag could play a nonspeaking role from one side of the stage.

PROPS

The hunter could be dressed appropriately in a plaid shirt or vest. The horse could be dressed in brown or black clothes. A saddle and bridle could be placed on the stage.

DELIVERY

The horse could sound frustrated at his predicament, both at the beginning and end of the fable. The hunter should sound persuasive.

CHARACTERS

📖	Narrator
HO	Horse
HU	Hunter
ST	Stag (nonspeaking, optional)

THE HORSE, THE HUNTER, AND THE STAG

Narrator: The horse and stag had an argument, and the stag ran off. The horse wanted to take revenge on the stag, so he came to the hunter to ask his help in finding him.

HO   **Horse:**   The stag thinks he has won our argument. How can I find him quickly? You are clever and wise and have many good ideas.   **1**

HU   **Hunter:**   Of course, I can help you, but first you must take this piece of iron between your jaws. Then I can guide you with these reins that I'll attach.   **2**

HO   **Horse:**   Do you really think all this is needed? All I want to do is take revenge on the stag.   **3**

HU   **Hunter:**   Be patient, my friend, for you first must find him. Let me put this saddle on your back so that I can steady myself while we look for him.   **4**

Narrator: The horse agreed, and the hunter soon bridled and saddled him. The horse even stood quietly while the hunter mounted him.

HU   **Hunter:**   Now that we are ready, let's find that stag.   **5**

Narrator: The hunter and horse soon overcame the stag.

HO   **Horse:**   Hunter, I thank you for your help. Now get off and remove those things from my mouth and back.   **6**

HU   **Hunter:**   Not so fast. Now that I have you bridled and saddled, I rather like having a horse to ride. I think I will keep you under my control.   **7**

Narrator: With those words, the sad horse learned his lesson:
If you allow people to use you for your own purposes, they also will use you for theirs.

From *Fifty Fabulous Fables*. © 1997 Suzanne I. Barchers. Teacher Ideas Press. (800) 237-6124.

THE KID AND THE FLUTE-PLAYING WOLF

SUMMARY

A flute-playing wolf captures a kid for its dinner. But when the kid convinces the wolf to play his flute, a pack of dogs hear the flute and scare off the wolf. (Aesop)

Reading level: 3.

PRESENTATION SUGGESTIONS

The narrator should stand off to the side, with the kid in the center and the wolf to one side. Non-speaking roles could be added by having dogs come onstage at the appropriate time.

PROPS

Consider displaying a pennywhistle or reed flute. The wolf could wear a tail and black T-shirt. The kid could be dressed in a beige T-shirt.

DELIVERY

The wolf should sound delighted at his good fortune in the beginning and resigned to his loss at the end. The kid should sound persuasive.

CHARACTERS

	Narrator
W	Wolf
K	Kid
D	Dogs (nonspeaking, optional)

THE KID AND THE FLUTE-PLAYING WOLF

Narrator: A kid had strayed from the flock and couldn't find its way back. Suddenly, a wolf came upon it.

Wolf: Aha! It looks like I have found my dinner! This is indeed my lucky day. I didn't even have to risk being seen by the dogs. **1**

Narrator: Now this was an unusual wolf. He loved to play the flute, and the kid saw the flute under the wolf's arm.

Kid: I see that I have no choice, Mr. Wolf, but to be your dinner. But why not do this dinner in style? Why don't you play your flute a bit, and I will dance. Then you can enjoy a truly fine evening. **2**

Wolf: Why, that sounds like a terrific idea. I'll just get my flute ready now. **3**

Narrator: The wolf played his flute, and the kid danced prettily about the grass. After a while, the noise of the flute attracted the attention of the dogs. They attacked the wolf, who had to run away and leave his dinner behind. As he ran, he shouted to the kid.

Wolf: *I got what I deserve.* After all, I'm really a butcher, not a flutist! **4**

From *Fifty Fabulous Fables*. © 1997 Suzanne I. Barchers. Teacher Ideas Press. (800) 237-6124.

THE LION AND THE WILD BOAR

SUMMARY

When a lion and a wild boar fight over who will get to drink from a spring, circling vultures convince them to make amends. (Aesop)
Reading level: 3.

PRESENTATION SUGGESTIONS

The lion and the boar should share center stage, with the narrator off to one side.

PROPS

The lion could wear a gold T-shirt, and the boar could wear a black T-shirt. A spring could be represented by a small pool or a circle cut out of aluminum foil. An outdoor setting could be portrayed with a mural, plants, rocks, and so forth.

DELIVERY

The lion and wild boar should sound argumentative and finally conciliatory.

CHARACTERS

    📖   Narrator
L   Lion
WB   Wild Boar

THE LION AND THE WILD BOAR

Narrator: On a very hot summer day, a lion and a wild boar came to drink at a spring. The spring was so small that they began to fight over who would get to drink from it.

L	**Lion:** This is where I always come to drink. By rights this spring is mine. Be off with you.	1
WB	**Wild Boar:** You may have drunk here in the past, but I got here first today. I am going to drink my fill, and you can have any that is left.	2
L	**Lion:** But the spring doesn't have enough for two. I'm sorry, my friend, but that springwater is mine.	3
WB	**Wild Boar:** You will have to kill me first to get that water.	4
L	**Lion:** That I will gladly do.	5

Narrator: The lion and the wild boar began to fight. They were evenly matched, and the fight went on and on. Soon it was clear that although one might kill the other, the survivor might die of exhaustion. The wild boar was on the ground, and the lion was ready to leap on him for the kill, when they heard the sound of vultures overhead.

WB	**Wild Boar:** Before you take that last leap, look above you, lion.	6

Narrator: The lion looked up and saw the vultures circling.

L	**Lion:** I think we would be wise to end this fight and share the water.	7
WB	**Wild Boar:** You are right, my friend. If we stop fighting, at least we will live to see another day.	8

Narrator: The two beasts took turns at the spring and went on their way, agreeing that: *Being friends was preferable to providing a meal for the vultures.*

From *Fifty Fabulous Fables*. © 1997 Suzanne I. Barchers. Teacher Ideas Press. (800) 237-6124.

THE LION, THE FOX, AND THE BEASTS

SUMMARY

A lion invites various animals into his cave to hear his will. When they don't come out again, the fox declines the lion's invitation. (Aesop)
Reading level: 3.

PRESENTATION SUGGESTIONS

The lion should dominate the stage but stand off to one side. As each animal is invited into the cave, it can disappear offstage. Students can lengthen this script by adding animals who go into the cave before the fox declines.

PROPS

The animals could wear labels or T-shirts in gold, gray, white, or black colors. A cave could be indicated with a mural.

DELIVERY

The lion should sound majestic. Except for the fox, the other animals should sound honored to be invited into the cave. The fox should sound wise.

CHARACTERS

📖	Narrator
L	Lion
G	Goat
S	Sheep
C	Calf
F	Fox

THE LION, THE FOX, AND THE BEASTS

 **Narrator:**   The majestic lion once sent out the news that he was dying. He asked all the animals in his kingdom to come and hear his will. The goat arrived first.

| L | **Lion:**   My friend, please come into my cave, and I will read you my will. | 1 |

| G | **Goat:**   Thank you for asking me. I am sorry to hear you aren't doing well. | 2 |

Narrator: The goat entered the cave but didn't come out. Finally the lion came out again and spoke to the sheep.

| L | **Lion:**   Madam sheep, please come into my cave, and I will read you my will. | 3 |

| S | **Sheep:**   Thank you for asking me, Your Majesty. I too am sorry to hear you aren't feeling well. | 4 |

Narrator: The sheep entered the cave but didn't come out. Finally the lion came out again and spoke to the calf.

| L | **Lion:**   Oh calf, please come into my cave, and I will read you my will. | 5 |

| C | **Calf:**   Thank you for asking me, Your Majesty. I heard from the others that you were doing poorly. | 6 |

Narrator: The calf entered the cave and also didn't come out. Finally the lion came out again and spoke to the fox.

L   **Lion:**   Why don't you come to hear my will and bid me good-bye   **7**
like the others?

F   **Fox:**   I beg your pardon, Your Majesty. But so many animals have   **8**
already come to see you. I see all their footprints going in, but none
coming out. Until the animals that entered your cave come out again,
I am going to stay out here.

Narrator: And with that the fox turned tail and left the lion alone.
The wise fox looks before he enters.

THE LION'S SHARE

SUMMARY

Four animals work together to kill a stag, but the lion claims the entire feast for himself. (Aesop)
Reading level: 3.

PRESENTATION SUGGESTIONS

The narrator should stand off center, with the lion dominating the stage, perhaps toward the front or on a stool. The jackal, fox, and wolf should sit or stand slightly behind the lion.

PROPS

The animals could wear appropriate felt or paper additions to distinguish them. Students could research the features of the jackal, fox, and wolf to determine the appropriate color and shape of ears, tails, and so forth.

DELIVERY

The lion should have a commanding voice, with the other animals reading in more moderate tones.

CHARACTERS

📖	Narrator
J	Jackal
F	Fox
W	Wolf
L	Lion

From *Fifty Fabulous Fables*. © 1997 Suzanne I. Barchers. Teacher Ideas Press. (800) 237-6124.

THE LION'S SHARE

Narrator: A lion went hunting with his friends, the fox, the jackal, and the wolf. They hunted and hunted.

J	**Jackal:** I am so hungry my stomach is rumbling.	1
F	**Fox:** I am so hungry my stomach is growling.	2
W	**Wolf:** I am so hungry my stomach is snarling.	3
L	**Lion:** Keep quiet. We'll find something soon.	4

Narrator: And so it was. They soon surprised a stag. The four animals worked together to chase the stag, surrounding and killing it. The four began to discuss how to divide it.

J	**Jackal:** I should be first. I am the most hungry.	5
W	**Wolf:** I need a large portion for I ran the hardest.	6
F	**Fox:** I want to take the most home. I have a family waiting for dinner.	7

Narrator: Then the lion stood over the deer. He told the others how it would be divided.

L   Lion: The first quarter is mine because I am King of the Beasts. The second quarter is mine because as king I make judgments. The third part comes to me because I helped in the chase. The fourth is mine because none of you dares to take it away.   **8**

Narrator: With that, the lion began to enjoy his meal. The others returned to their dens with their empty stomachs. Don't ever forget this story. *The great will always let you help with the work. But they may not let you share in the reward.*

From *Fifty Fabulous Fables*. © 1997 Suzanne I. Barchers. Teacher Ideas Press. (800) 237-6124.

THE MAN, THE BOY, AND THE DONKEY

SUMMARY

When a father and son take their donkey to the market, people passing by chastise them in turn for having the son ride, having the father ride, and having both ride. Finally, they give the donkey a ride, with tragic results. (Aesop)
Reading level: 3.

PRESENTATION SUGGESTIONS

This script provides opportunities for many participants to have parts. In addition to those indicated, students could double up with the men and women who meet the father and son. The father and son should be in center stage, with the other people passing by as they comment on the donkey.

PROPS

The characters could be dressed as country folk. Consider creating a rural scene with plants, a mural, a brown paper path, and so forth.

DELIVERY

The country folk should sound outraged at the treatment of the donkey.

CHARACTERS

📖	Narrator	**M2**	Man Two
M1	Man One	**W2**	Woman Two
F	Father	**M3**	Man Three
S	Son	**W3**	Woman Three
W1	Woman One		

THE MAN, THE BOY, AND THE DONKEY

 Narrator: A father and son were going to the market with their donkey. As they were walking along, a man saw them and stopped.

M1   **Man One:**   Why are you walking when you have a donkey to ride? You must be very foolish not to use this animal for what it is intended.   **1**

F   **Father:**   That man makes sense, son. Why don't you ride the donkey to the market?   **2**

S   **Son:**   Thank you, father. I'll just ride for a while.   **3**

 Narrator: The son climbed onto the donkey, and they continued on their way. Soon a woman stopped them.

W1   **Woman One:**   Shame on that lazy child. He rides the donkey and lets his father walk.   **4**

S   **Son:**   She's right, Father. I'll walk now.   **5**

 Narrator: So the boy climbed down from the donkey, and the man got on to ride to the market. They walked along farther and soon met a man and a woman.

M2   **Man Two:**   Look at that lazy man! He rides while the child walks.   **6**

W2   **Woman Two:**   That poor little boy! He must be so tired.   **7**

 Narrator: The man didn't know what to do. He stopped for a moment and thought.

F   **Father:**   Son, climb up here with me. We'll ride together.   **8**

Narrator: The man and his son rode together on their donkey to the market. By the time they got close, people began to point at them.

M3   **Man Three:**   Look at how they both ride that poor, tired donkey.   **9**

W3   **Woman Three:**   They should be ashamed of themselves! That donkey looks like it is about to drop.   **10**

Narrator: The father and son climbed off and tried to decide what to do next.

S   **Son:**   People scold us when I ride and let you walk.   **11**

F   **Father:**   And they scold us when I ride and let you walk.   **12**

S   **Son:**   And they scold us when we both ride.   **13**

F   **Father:**   Maybe we should let the donkey ride for a while.   **14**

Narrator: So they cut down a pole, tied the donkey's feet to it, and carried the donkey along to the market. This caused all the people to point and laugh, but the father and son continued. When they got to the market bridge, the donkey kicked loose of the pole, and the boy dropped his end. Trying to get free, the donkey fell over the bridge. With two feet still tied together he drowned.

S   **Son:**   Well, I guess we learned a lesson, Father.   **15**

F   **Father:**   What is that, son?   **16**

S   **Son:**   *You can't please everyone.*   **17**

THE MILKMAID AND HER PAIL

SUMMARY

A young girl takes a pail of milk to market, thinking about how she will spend the money she earns. She learns through experience that she shouldn't count her chickens before they're hatched. (Aesop)
Reading level: 3.

PRESENTATION SUGGESTIONS

The milkmaid has the primary role and should be center stage. The mother could exit after the beginning and return for the ending.

PROPS

The mother could be dressed in an apron and shawl. The girl could wear a ruffled apron or dress. A pail could be on the stage.

DELIVERY

The mother should sound kind. The daughter should sound dreamy when talking about what she'll buy and petulant when referring to Polly Shaw.

CHARACTERS

📖   Narrator
M   Mother
D   Daughter

THE MILKMAID AND HER PAIL

Narrator: A mother lived with her young daughter. The daughter was foolish but kindhearted. One day the mother sent the daughter to the market with a pail of milk.

M   **Mother:** Daughter, take this pail of milk to the market.   **1**

D   **Daughter:** Yes, mother. And what shall I do with the money? Shall I do some shopping for you?   **2**

M   **Mother:** Bring half of it home for me. You may spend the other half.   **3**

Narrator: The daughter was happy at the thought of having some money to spend. She put the pail of milk on her head and set off down the path to the market. She thought about what she would do with her share of the money.

D   **Daughter:** I know what I will do. First I will buy some chickens from Farmer Brown. They will lay eggs each morning. Then I will sell the eggs to the preacher's wife.   **4**

Narrator: She continued down the path thinking about the money she would earn from those eggs.

D   **Daughter:** I'll use the money from selling the eggs to buy a new dress and hat. When I go to the market next time, all the young men will speak to me. Won't that just make Polly Shaw mad! But I won't care. I'll just look at her and toss my head—just like this!   **5**

Narrator: She tossed her head back, and the pail fell off. All the milk was spilled. Sadly, she went home and told her mother what she had done.

M   **Mother:** Ah, my poor child. Now you have learned an important lesson: *Do not count your chickens before they are hatched.*   **6**

From *Fifty Fabulous Fables.* © 1997 Suzanne I. Barchers. Teacher Ideas Press. (800) 237-6124.

THE TREE AND THE REED

SUMMARY

A tree and a reed argue over who is safest. The tree learns that even the mighty can come to a sad end. (Aesop)
Reading level: 3.

PRESENTATION SUGGESTIONS

The tree could be center stage with the reader sitting on a high stool. The reed could perform from a low stool or from the floor. The narrator should be off to the side. This fable could be paired with "The Wind and the Sun" on page 115.

PROPS

Consider using tree branches, reeds, or other similar materials. The pond could be indicated by aluminum foil, colored paper, or crayoned paper on the floor.

DELIVERY

The tree should sound bold and authoritative. The reed could sound smaller, yet self-assured.

CHARACTERS

📖	Narrator
T	Tree
R	Reed

THE TREE AND THE REED

Narrator: The tree and the reed lived side by side near a lovely pond. They often enjoyed passing the time of day in conversation. On this day the tree was taunting the reed.

T	**Tree:** Why don't you plant your feet deeply in the ground as I do? Then you could raise your head high in the air.	**1**
R	**Reed:** I'm quite content with how things are. It is true, I'm not as grand as you are. But I think I am safer where I am.	**2**
T	**Tree:** You don't think I am safe? What could possibly come along and pluck me up by the roots? Who could make my head bow to the ground?	**3**
R	**Reed:** Just the same, dear friend, I think I am content to be what I am.	**4**

Narrator: Some time later a hurricane arose. The winds blew and blew, uprooting the tree and flinging it to the ground. The tree would never again have the majesty of its past.

R	**Reed:** My dear friend, it hurts me to see you upon the ground. But now you can see that being able to bend with the wind can be better than having deep roots and a high head.	**5**

Narrator: The tree agreed, learning all too late that: *Being small often brings safety.*

From *Fifty Fabulous Fables*. © 1997 Suzanne I. Barchers. Teacher Ideas Press. (800) 237-6124.

THE WIND AND THE SUN

SUMMARY

The wind and the sun argue about who is the strongest, settling their argument through a contest. (Aesop)
Reading level: 3.

PRESENTATION SUGGESTIONS

The wind and the sun should dominate the stage, with the narrator and traveler off to either side. The traveler could be offstage until the appropriate time. For an additional nonspeaking role, a cloud could be added for the sun to hide behind. Add wind sounds through audience participation.

PROPS

The wind and the sun could be costumed, or the wind could wear a white T-shirt while the sun wears a gold T-shirt. The traveler should be dressed in a coat that he or she could take off at the appropriate time.

DELIVERY

The wind should sound blustery and loud. The sun should also sound assertive and confident. The traveler should sound cold and then hot.

CHARACTERS

📖	Narrator
W	Wind
S	Sun
T	Traveler
C	Cloud (nonspeaking, optional)

THE WIND AND THE SUN

Narrator: The wind and the sun were usually good friends. But on this day, they were having an argument.

W   **Wind:** I know you think you are strong, dear Sun, but look at how hard I can blow. I am definitely the stronger one.   **1**

S   **Sun:** But think about what my rays can do. How can you ignore how hot I can make it?   **2**

Narrator: The wind and the sun continued to argue until they saw a traveler coming down the road.

W   **Wind:** I know how we can settle this. Let's have a contest.   **3**

S   **Sun:** Good idea! The person who can make that traveler take off his coat will prove that he is the stronger one.   **4**

W   **Wind:** That sounds fair. I'll begin.   **5**

Narrator: The sun hid behind a cloud, and the wind began to blow hard at the traveler.

T   **Traveler:** Oh, it has gotten so windy all of a sudden! Where did the sun go? I'm glad I have this warm coat, even though it's hard to keep it on in this strong wind.   **6**

W   **Wind:** See, even he says I am strong.   **7**

S   **Sun:** But look how tightly he keeps his coat pulled on.   **8**

Narrator: So the wind blew even harder. And the traveler just pulled the coat more firmly around him. Finally, the wind gave up.

S   **Sun:**   Now it's my turn. Remember to stay calm, my friend.   **9**

Narrator: The sun came out from behind the cloud and shone down on the traveler.

T   **Traveler:**   What happened to the wind? It has turned so warm that I think I can take my coat off.   **10**

Narrator: The traveler removed his coat and the sun won the contest, proving that: *Kindness is better than cruelty.*

PART 4

ANDROCLES

SUMMARY

When an escaped slave helps a lion with a thorn in its paw, the lion returns the favor. (Aesop)
Reading level: 4.

PRESENTATION SUGGESTIONS

In keeping with the nature of this classic tale, the lion's role is nonspeaking. However, its presence is vital to the tale and should be maintained on-stage. Determine when the lion should mime its pain and behavior so that the story maintains its dignity. Androcles and the lion should have prominent positions on the stage, with the narrator to one side. The master and emperor could enter later for their roles or stay on the other side of the stage.

PROPS

The person playing the lion could hold a stick between two fingers, representing the thorn. A rag could be used to bind up the paw. A mural could represent the cave and forest. The emperor could have a crown.

DELIVERY

Androcles should have a quiet, caring delivery. The master should sound angry, and the emperor should sound regal.

CHARACTERS

Narrator
Androcles
Lion (nonspeaking)
Master
Emperor

ANDROCLES

Narrator: Androcles was a slave who escaped from his master. He fled into the forest but soon lost his way. As he wandered about, he came upon a lion. The lion was lying down and moaning with pain. Instead of running away in fear, Androcles stood and watched for a moment.

Androcles: That lion looks to be in terrible pain. I wonder what is wrong with it. There, it sees me, but it doesn't even move.   1

Narrator: With that, Androcles moved closer.

Androcles: Why, you have a huge thorn in your paw. That is what is causing you such pain. Stay quiet, and I shall try to remove it.   2

Narrator: Androcles leaned against the lion and gently worked the huge thorn out of the lion's paw.

Androcles: That is better. Now I'll wrap it for you with this piece of my shirt. It should heal quickly.   3

Narrator: The lion gently pulled at Androcles's arm. Ignoring his earlier fear, Androcles let the lion pull him to a cave. Androcles hid there, and the lion brought him meat every day. But one day hunters came to the wood and captured the lion. When Androcles went out to search for his friend, he was captured by his master.

Master: Androcles, you must pay for your escape. I am taking you to the emperor, who will make judgment and decide your punishment.   4

Narrator: The emperor heard the master's complaint.

Emperor: Slave, you must suffer for your escape. You will be thrown to   **5**
a hungry lion. This lesson will show other slaves that they cannot hope to
escape and live.

Narrator: The emperor, master, and all of the court came to see the
punishment. Androcles was placed in the middle of the arena. Then a lion
was set loose from its cage. It rushed toward Androcles, ready to tear him
apart. Then it stopped and began to lick Androcles' hands.

Androcles: My friend! How good it is to see you again!   **6**

Narrator: The emperor was astonished at this unexpected turn of events.

Emperor: What is this! Slave, come to me! Why is this lion treating   **7**
you like a master?

Androcles: Your Highness, when I was in the woods, I came upon this   **8**
beast, who was suffering from a thorn in its paw. I removed the thorn, and
the lion kept me well fed in its cave. When it did not return one day, I
went in search of it and was captured.

Emperor: Well, it seems that you showed great bravery and that the   **9**
lion knows that: *Gratitude is the sign of noble souls.*

Narrator: And with that, the emperor pardoned Androcles and set the
lion loose in its forest; both received their rewards for noble acts.

THE ANT AND THE GRASSHOPPER

SUMMARY

In this well-known fable, the ant toils through the summer while the grasshopper plays. Later, the grasshopper discovers that he should have been working during the summer too. (Aesop)
Reading level: 4.

PRESENTATION SUGGESTIONS

The narrator could stand to the side with the grasshopper in the center. The ant could pass by at the appropriate moments. To involve more students, have several ants working and responding.

PROPS

The ants could be dressed in black, with the grasshopper in green or light brown. If possible, place an ear of corn on the stage.

DELIVERY

The grasshopper should sound playful and carefree. The ant should sound efficient.

CHARACTERS

Narrator
Grasshopper
Ant(s)

THE ANT AND THE GRASSHOPPER

Narrator: It was a lovely summer day. A grasshopper was hopping about, chirping, singing, and enjoying the sunshine. Meanwhile, the ant passed by, carrying an ear of corn that he was taking to his nest for the long winter months.

Grasshopper: You are working too hard, dear ant. Take a break and come and chat with me.

Ant: I am working so hard because winter will be here before we know it. You should also take some time to put food away before it is too late.

Grasshopper: I'm not worried about the winter. There's plenty of food for now. This sun won't be here soon, and I'm not going to miss it.

Narrator: The grasshopper kept playing, and the ant kept working. Soon summer ended and winter came. The grasshopper had no food and found himself dying of hunger. He appealed to the ant for help.

Grasshopper: My friend, I am dying of hunger. Can you spare a bit of food for a hungry grasshopper?

Ant: If you remember, I advised you to end your playing and store some food away for the winter. If I share with you, then my family will go hungry. I am sorry, grasshopper, but my family comes first.

Narrator: And with this, the grasshopper learned a sad lesson: *It is best to prepare for the days of need.*

1

2

3

4

5

From *Fifty Fabulous Fables.* © 1997 Suzanne I. Barchers. Teacher Ideas Press. (800) 237-6124.

THE FOX AND THE MONKEY WHO WAS ELECTED KING

SUMMARY

The fox is jealous when the monkey is elected king. He tricks him into being caught in a trap, proving that the monkey is not worthy of being king. (Aesop)
Reading level: 4.

PRESENTATION SUGGESTIONS

This play offers an opportunity for many animals to participate briefly. The fox and the monkey should stand in center stage, with the narrator on one side and the animals on the other side. Consider adding music, in the beginning or as fanfare at the animals' lines.

PROPS

Let students choose their animals and create their own costumes. The kid, fox, and monkey should be distinguished from the other animals.

DELIVERY

The monkey should sound enthusiastic and then outraged. The fox should sound clever.

CHARACTERS

Narrator

Kid

Animals

Fox

Monkey

THE FOX AND THE MONKEY
WHO WAS ELECTED KING

Narrator: The animals all got together for an evening of fun. Everyone enjoyed the monkey's dancing. Soon it came time to elect a new king, and the kid suggested that the monkey be made king.

Kid: Let's make the monkey our new king. He is the best dancer of all of us. We would have many grand evenings with him as king.   1

Animals: Yes! Yes! Monkey for king! Monkey for king!   2

Narrator: The monkey became king, but the fox was jealous. He found a piece of meat set out in a trap by hunters. He went to the monkey to trick him into being caught in the trap.

Fox: Your Highness, I have found a great treasure that truly belongs to you.   3

Monkey: That sounds wonderful. Where is this treasure?   4

Fox: Follow me. I will take you to it.   5

Narrator: When the monkey saw the meat, he rushed into the trap and was caught. He was very angry at the fox for tricking him.

Monkey: You tricked me, fox!   6

Fox: One who can be so easily tricked does not deserve to be king.   7

Narrator: Thus the fox proved to the animals that: *Wisdom is more important than dancing.*

From *Fifty Fabulous Fables*. © 1997 Suzanne I. Barchers. Teacher Ideas Press. (800) 237-6124.

THE MAN AND THE NIGHTINGALE

SUMMARY

When a man hears a nightingale singing, he decides to capture it. The nightingale convinces the man to let it go, teaching him three valuable lessons in exchange. (Aesop) A Russian version by Ivan Krylov replaces the man with a cat, who also captures the bird. When the bird can't trill in the cat's grasp, the cat eats it. Consider having students revise the story to match this version.

Reading level: 4.

PRESENTATION SUGGESTIONS

The man could sit center stage on a chair, with the nightingale perched on a stool above him. The narrator could stand off to one side. Consider opening the story with bird calls or flute music.

PROPS

The man could be dressed simply. Students could create a simple nightingale cage or bring a bamboo birdcage for the stage.

DELIVERY

The nightingale should sound persuasive.

CHARACTERS

Narrator

Man

Nightingale

THE MAN AND THE NIGHTINGALE

Narrator: A man listened to a nightingale singing throughout a warm summer's night. Rather than being disturbed by the singing, he found it quite pleasant. He decided to capture the nightingale so he could listen to its singing all the time.

Man: I'll make a trap for that little bird. Then I'll never be lonely again.   **1**

Narrator: The man created a clever trap, and the next day he caught the nightingale.

Nightingale: Why have you captured me?   **2**

Man: I love listening to you sing. Now I can listen to you at any time.   **3**

Nightingale: Don't you know that nightingales never sing when they are in a cage?   **4**

Man: Then I guess I will have to eat you. I've heard that nightingales make a small but tasty meal.   **5**

Nightingale: I am not worth killing and eating. Set me free, and I will tell you three things worth a lot more than my little body.   **6**

Man: I doubt that you know three things so important.   **7**

Nightingale: Don't forget that I fly to many places. I learn of many things in my travels.   **8**

From *Fifty Fabulous Fables.* © 1997 Suzanne I. Barchers. Teacher Ideas Press. (800) 237-6124.

Man: All right, then. I'll set you free.   **9**

Narrator: The man opened the cage and the nightingale flew to a high branch of a tree.

Man: Now tell me those three things, nightingale.   **10**

Nightingale: First, never believe a promise given by someone in a cage.   **11**

Man: I have surely learned that lesson!   **12**

Nightingale: Second, keep what you already have.   **13**

Man: Aha! You are right about that, too.   **14**

Nightingale: Third, don't be sad over what you've lost forever.   **15**

Narrator: And then the nightingale flew away, and the man never heard its lovely song again.

APPENDIX: A FABLES UNIT

A BRIEF HISTORY OF FABLES

The fables of Aesop are most familiar to schoolchildren. Aesop was a slave at Samos in Greece during the epoch of the Tyrants, approximately 550 B.C. It was politically dangerous to speak freely during this period, and fables were shared to communicate veiled meanings. In later years, when free speech was acceptable, the popularity of fables continued. Aesop's fables were written by Demetrius of Phaleron, founder of the Alexandria Library, in about 300 B.C. (Jacobs 1966, xv–xvi).

Collections of Indian fables include *The Panchatantra,* meaning "five books," and *The Jatakas,* "a Buddhist name for stories concerning the rebirths of Gautama Buddha, who according to tradition was reincarnated many times in the forms of different animals until he became at last Buddha, the Enlightened One" (Arbuthnot and Sutherland 1972, 188). Jean de La Fontaine (1621–1695) published beautifully written fables that became so popular he was called *le fablier,* "the fable-teller" (ibid.). Ethel Heins has brought us Russian fables in *The Cat and the Cook and Other Fables of Krylov* (1995).

ELEMENTS OF FABLES

Fables often feature a trickster who endeavors to expose another character as a fool. If the trickster is not himself duped in one fable, he often is victim in a subsequent fable. Fables combine unlikely animal characters: fox and crow, tortoise and hare, frog and bull, fox and stork. Traditional fables are short, presenting a simple problem or conflict, often followed by a moral or lesson. If a lesson or moral is not stated directly, it is always implied. In addition to traditional collections of Aesop's or La Fontaine's fables, one can find contemporary versions with beautiful illustrations.

PREPARING THE UNIT

Gather together enough collections or picture books of fables so each student can use one. A set of ten copies of Arnold Lobel's *Fables* is highly recommended because students especially enjoy reading these. (Alternatively, Lobel's tales could be shared orally.)

Before reading any fable aloud, read them carefully to yourself. Some of the morals might be too difficult for your students, the language could be too dated, or the context may be inappropriate. Be sure to intersperse the traditional collections, such as Joseph Jacobs's, with the illustrated collections, such as Eric Carle's.

INTRODUCING THE UNIT

Read aloud several fables in the traditional style of the collections by David Levine, Joseph Jacobs, or Roger L'Estrange. After sharing several examples, have students predict the moral or lesson. Contrast Levine's fables, which do not include morals, with fables in Jacobs and L'Estrange. For beginning or remedial readers, set up a listening center with books and cassettes obtained from the Society for Visual Instruction (SVE). Titles at a 1.5 (approximately first grade, fifth month) reading level include: *The Fox and the Crow,*

The Town Mouse and the Country Mouse, The Fox and the Grapes, The Boy Who Cried Wolf, and *The Crow and the Pitcher.* SVE also offers a video that includes *The Country Mouse and the Town Mouse, The Fox and the Grapes, The Boy Who Cried Wolf, The Tortoise and the Hare,* and *The Wolf in Sheep's Clothing*, along with a parent's kit of Aesop's fables that includes the VHS cassette and activity cards. Obtain a catalog from SVE by calling 1-800-829-1900.

Review the fables that were shared and write the morals on a piece of chart paper. If morals were not included, decide on a moral and list it. Keep this list and add to it throughout the unit. Have students decide how to record the fables they have read and heard. Possibilities include a log, a journal, charts, or note cards. Help students keep up their records during the course of the unit.

SUGGESTED ACTIVITIES

In addition to the readers theatre scripts, the following activities can be used as a base for the unit. Many activities could be described on cards for student use, and individuals or small groups can choose which ones to pursue. Encourage students to devise additional activities and explorations throughout the course of the unit; when they do, add them to your activity suggestions.

Comparing Traditional Fables Retold by Contemporary Author/Illustrators

Continue to read additional traditional fables. Next, have students explore Jack Kent's and Eric Carle's collections. Then share Janet Stevens's version of *The Tortoise and the Hare*. Point out how these authors retell the tales in a more contemporary style. Examine Stevens's illustrations for modern touches such as the tortoise's sandals and tennis shoes. Suggest that students work in small groups to compare the modern aspects to the traditional in these versions or others they can locate. The comparisons could be shown through an attribute or classification chart.

Contemporary Fables

Share several of Arnold Lobel's *Fables* and parallel traditional examples. Start a new chart and begin listing Lobel's morals. Ask students how the fables differ and list the differences on the board. Then discuss the similarities. The students can work in small groups and classify the differences and similarities between Lobel and, for example, Jacobs. Groups need to decide how to chart the comparisons and how to share their results with the entire class.

Tissue Paper Art

Carle uses brightly colored tissue paper and paint for his illustrations. Explore the pattern of the endpapers in his book. Students can experiment with a simple form of tissue art by cutting tissue paper in various shapes and arranging them in overlays. When they are pleased with the interplay of colors and arrangement, they can glue the tissue in place. Students can explore other illustration techniques and experiment with additional media.

Creating Wordless Fables

Students can explore Ed Young's *The Other Bone* and then read a traditional version of the fable ("The Dog and the Shadow" in Jacobs's collection). Discuss how Young tells the entire story without words and clearly shows the beginning, middle, and end. Brainstorm fables that could be illustrated without words: "The Grasshopper and the Ant," "The Country Mouse and the City Mouse," and "The Lion and the Mouse." Students, individually or in pairs, can create wordless picture books for a fable of their choice.

Fable Characters and New Stories

Review traditional fables and list the featured characters: dog, lion, rooster, fox, crow, wolf, mice, crane, bull, donkey, birds, frog, horse, hare, goat, serpent, ox, bat, ant, grasshopper, cat, turtle or tortoise, bear, and so forth. Brainstorm new connections between the animals that could serve as new story ideas. Students can work in small groups to create new connections and share them with the whole class.

Fable Themes

Discuss how themes such as flattery, fear, rescue, and revenge occur in fables. Review fables that have been read and list as many themes as possible. Students can then look through fable collections and find new examples of each theme, choosing a way to represent their findings. Possible themes include courage, fear, rescue, revenge, little against big, trickery, conceit, friends or enemies, envy, greed, gratitude, and flattery.

Writing Individual Fables

Discuss with students the aspects of writing their own fables. Discuss the themes, characters, settings, problems, and morals that have been analyzed. Work together to create new characters or combinations of characters and brainstorm ideas for settings, themes, and problems. It isn't necessary that all elements be different but that the fable be new in some regard. Students may imply a moral or state it. After students have created their first draft, share the fables and guide revisions. Prepare the fables for publication in a class set or have students individually illustrate them. Students can then adapt their fables into readers theatre scripts.

Culminating Activity and Evaluation: Fables Afternoon

To prepare for an afternoon of sharing fables, have students choose to work in small groups that might share the following with guests: charts created while comparing traditional fables with contemporary retellings; examples of artwork inspired by Eric Carle; a display of students' wordless fables; a chart of fable themes; readers theatre scripts. Small groups should meet and plan how to display or explain their choice. Groups can have individual tables and visitors can rotate through the displays. After browsing, visitors can be seated and listen to the students perform readers theatre scripts. Because the fables are short, there should be adequate time to hear all students in performance.

On the following day, spend time reviewing the various activities of the unit. Ask students to evaluate their choices and their additions. Have them reflect on what they enjoyed the most, what they learned, and what they would recommend for other classes. Keep a record of their observations for the next time you explore fables.

REFERENCES

Arbuthnot, May Hill, and Zena Sutherland. *Children and Books.* 4th edition. Glenview, IL: Scott, Foresman and Company, 1972.

Jacobs, Joseph, editor. *The Fables of Aesop.* Illustrated by Richard Heighway. New York: Schocken Books, 1966. First published in 1894.

BIBLIOGRAPHY

FABLES

Alborough, Jez. *The Grass Is Always Greener.* New York: Dial Books for Young Readers, 1987. Grades one and up.
   Lincoln, a lamb, continues to frolic when Thomas leads the others up the hill in search of greener grass.

Anno, Mitsumasa. *Anno's Aesop: A Book of Fables by Aesop and Mr. Fox.* New York: Orchard Books, 1987. Grades one and up.
   More than forty traditional fables are interspersed with new tales read by Mr. Fox to his son.

Caldecott, Randolph, and Alfred Caldecott. *The Caldecott Aesop.* New York: Doubleday, 1978. Originally published in 1883 by Macmillan Co., London. Grades one and up.
   Though the original version is more than 100 years old, this collection of twenty tales is easily read and has pleasant color illustrations.

Calmenson, Stephanie, reteller. *The Children's Aesop.* Illustrated by Robert Byrd. Honesdale, PA: Caroline House, 1992. Grades one and up.
   Twenty-eight retellings are highlighted with colorfully decorative illustrations.

Carle, Eric, reteller. *Twelve Tales from Aesop.* New York: Philomel Books, 1980. Grades one and up.
   Carle's easy-to-read retellings and full-color illustrations provide an attractive collection of fables.

Galdone, Paul. *Three Aesop Fox Fables.* New York: Clarion Books, 1971. Grades one and up.
   "The Fox and the Grapes," "The Fox and the Stork," and "The Fox and the Crow" are Galdone's selections for this beautifully illustrated picture book.

Hague, Michael, editor. *Aesop's Fables.* New York: Holt, Rinehart & Winston, 1985. Grades one and up.
   Hague has selected and illustrated thirteen familiar fables in this beautiful collection.

Heins, Ethel. *The Cat and the Cook and Other Fables of Krylov.* New York: Greenwillow Books, 1995. Grades one and up.
   Heins has retold twelve Russian fables. Includes beautiful illustrations.

Jacobs, Joseph, editor. *The Fables of Aesop.* Illustrated by Richard Heighway. New York: Schocken Books, 1966. First published in 1894. Grades two and up.
   More than eighty fables are collected and illustrated with black-and-white line drawings.

Kent, Jack. *Fables of Aesop.* New York: Parents Magazine Press, 1972. Grades one and up.
   Thirteen fables are told in the simplest form available. Color illustrations enhance Kent's retellings. These are appropriate for the earliest reader.

L'Estrange, Roger. *Fables of Aesop.* Illustrated by Alexander Calder. New York: Dover Publications, 1967. Grades three and up.
   Sir Roger L'Estrange is the reteller of Aesop's fables, dated 1692. The stories are told simply, but the spelling has been retained, making the reading more challenging. The simple line drawings might inspire young artists.

Levine, David, editor and illustrator. *The Fables of Aesop.* Translated by Patrick and Justina Gregory. Harvard and Boston, MA: Harvard Common Press, 1975. Grades three and up.
    One hundred fables are presented with black-and-white line drawings. The stories are told in a simple style.

Lobel, Arnold. *Fables.* New York: Harper & Row, 1980. Grades one and up.
    Lobel has written twenty irreverent contemporary fables that children find particularly delightful.

Stevens, Janet. *The Tortoise and the Hare.* New York: Holiday House, 1984. Grades one and up.
    Stevens's color illustrations have a contemporary look, and her adaptation is full of humor.

Young, Ed. *The Other Bone.* New York: Harper & Row, 1984. Grades kindergarten and up.
    Young uses black-and-white drawings to illustrate this wordless version of the dog who loses his bone when he sees his reflection in a pool.

Zwerger, Lisbeth. *Aesop's Fables.* Saxonville, MA: Picture Book Studio, 1989. Grades two and up.
    Delicate wash and ink illustrations grace twelve well-known fables.

FILMS

Aesop's Fables. McGraw, 1967.
    Victor Borge reads seven fables in this thirteen-minute-long color film. Also available on video.

Fox and the Rooster. Encyclopaedia Britannica, 1951.
    Farm and forest animals are used to illustrate Aesop's fables in this black-and-white film.

ALPHABETICAL INDEX TO TALES

ABOUT THE AUTHOR

Suzanne I. Barchers received her bachelor of science degree in elementary education from Eastern Illinois University, her master's degree in education in reading from Oregon State University, and her doctor of education degree in curriculum and instruction from the University of Colorado, Boulder.

Ms. Barchers has been an educator and administrator for more than twenty years. She is a contributing author to *Learning* and *Mailbox Bookbag* magazines. She is on the affiliate faculty at the University of Colorado, Denver, and works in publishing. This is her ninth book.